MANSA MUSA COLORING BOOK

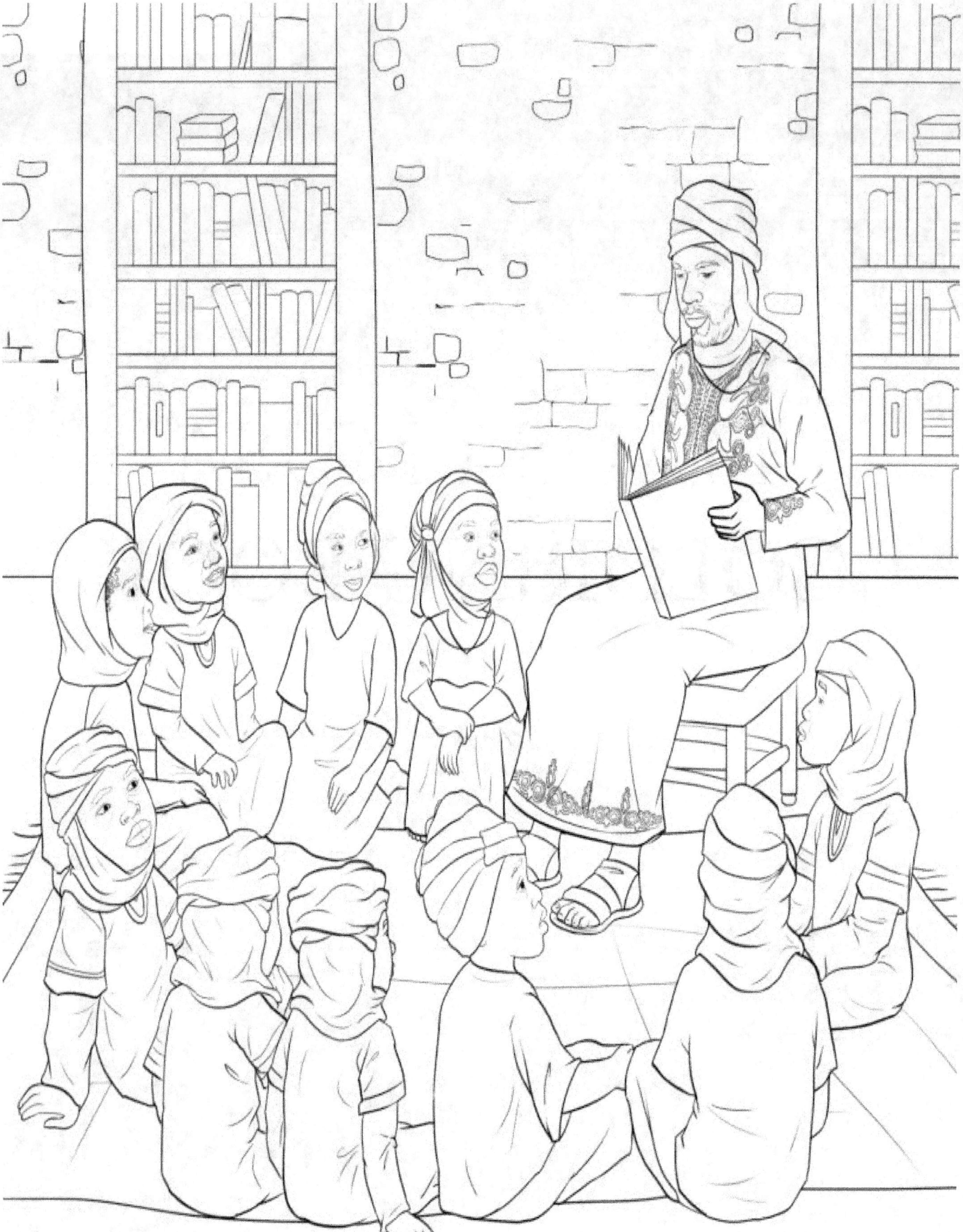

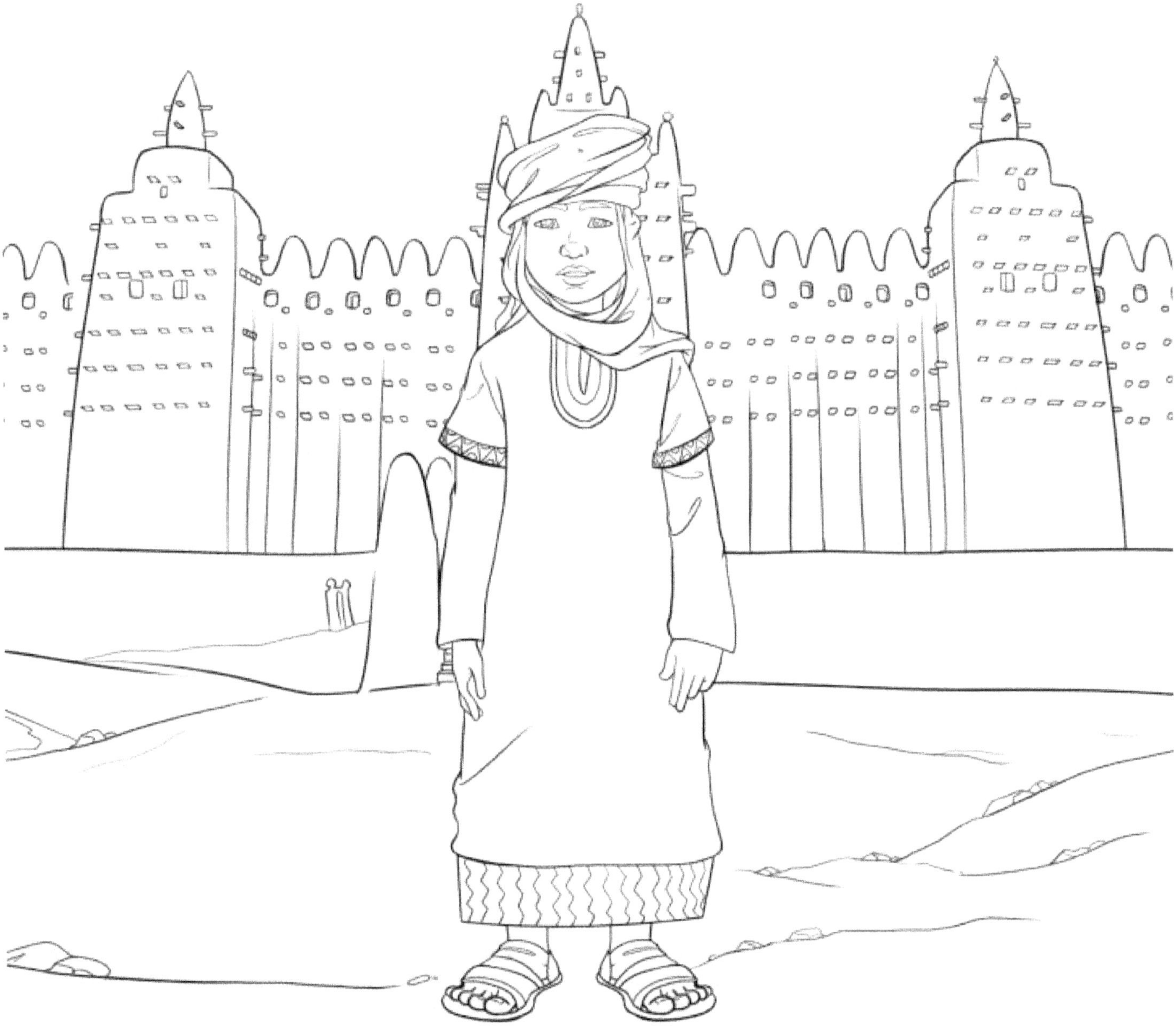

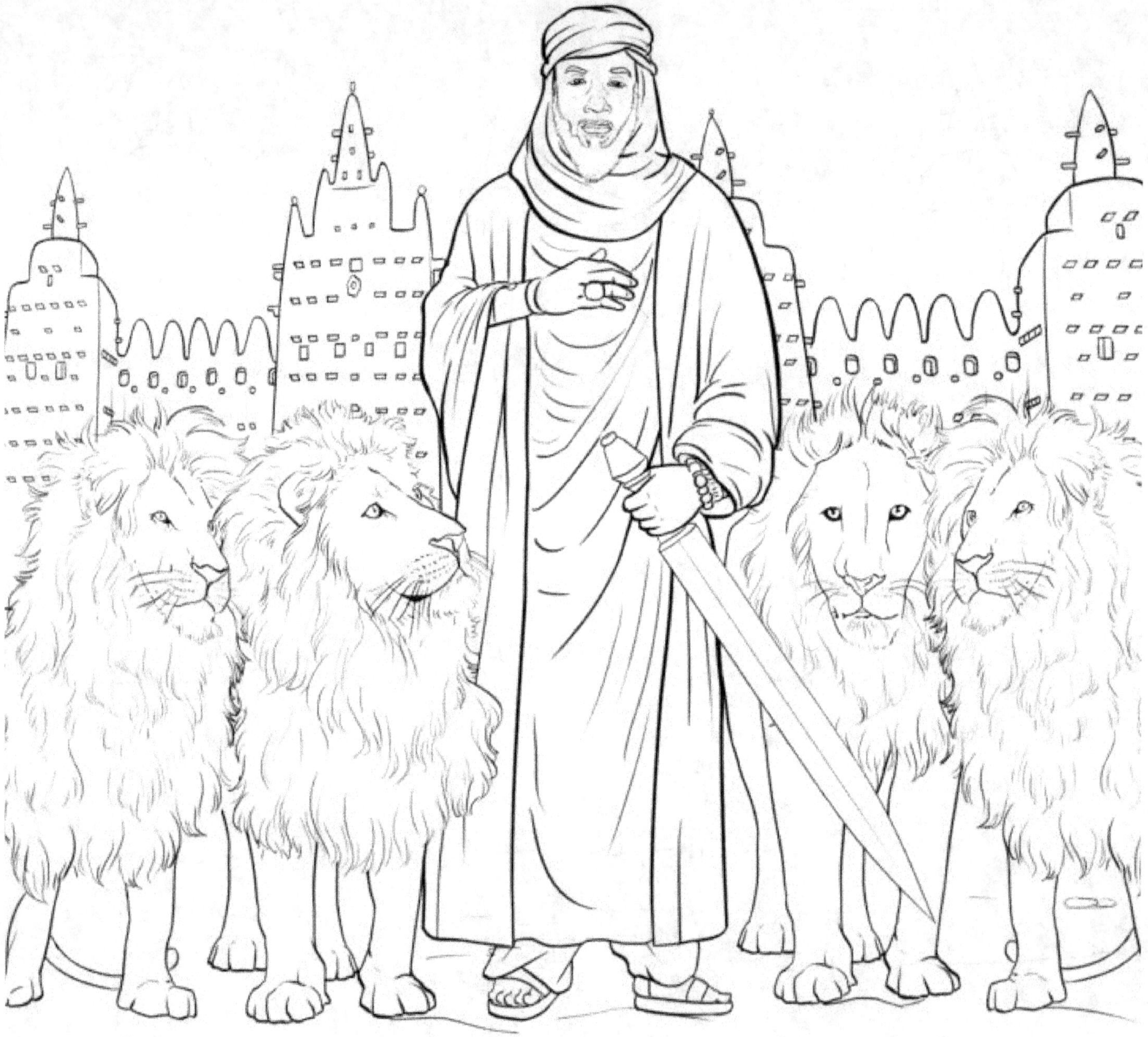

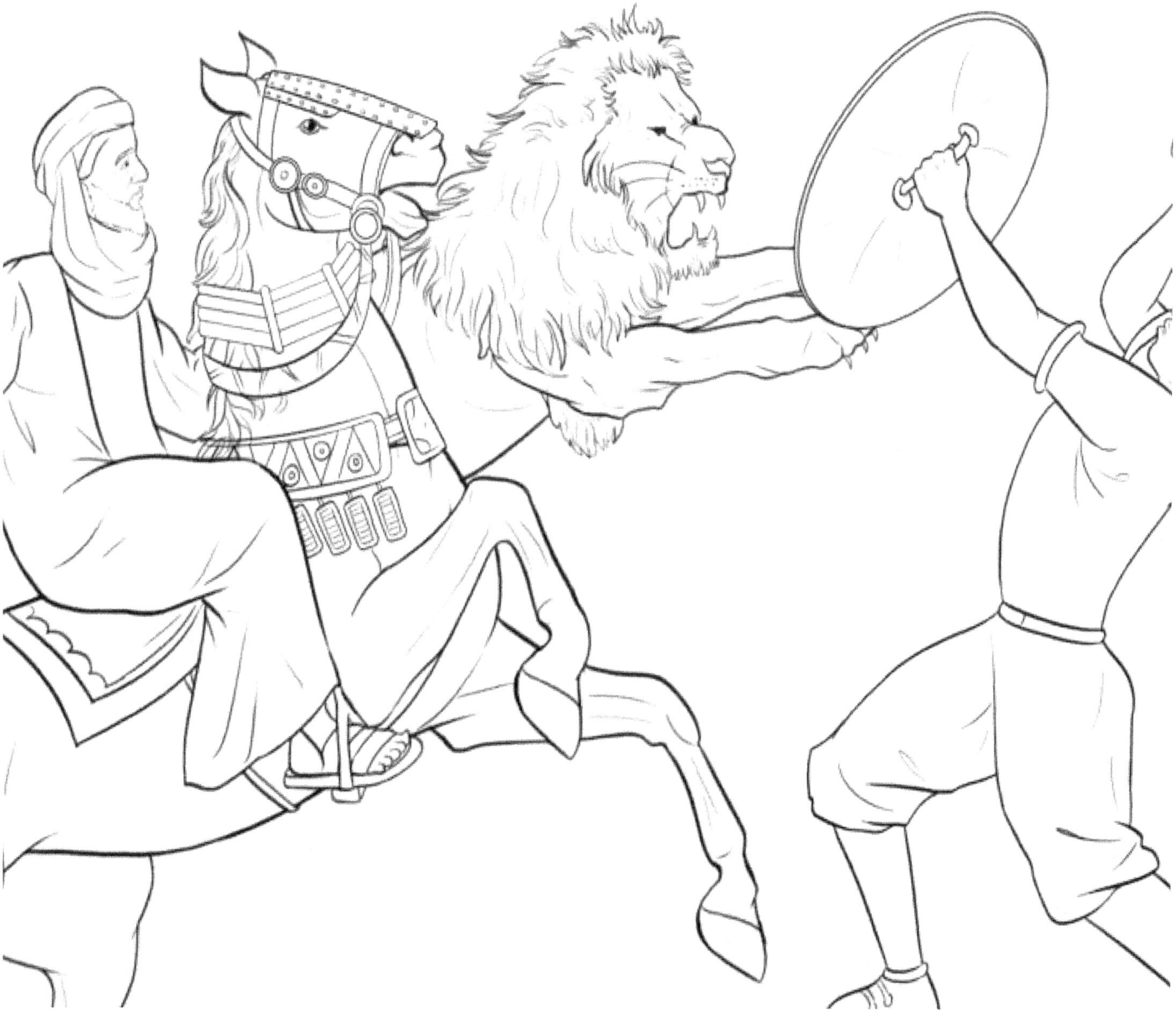

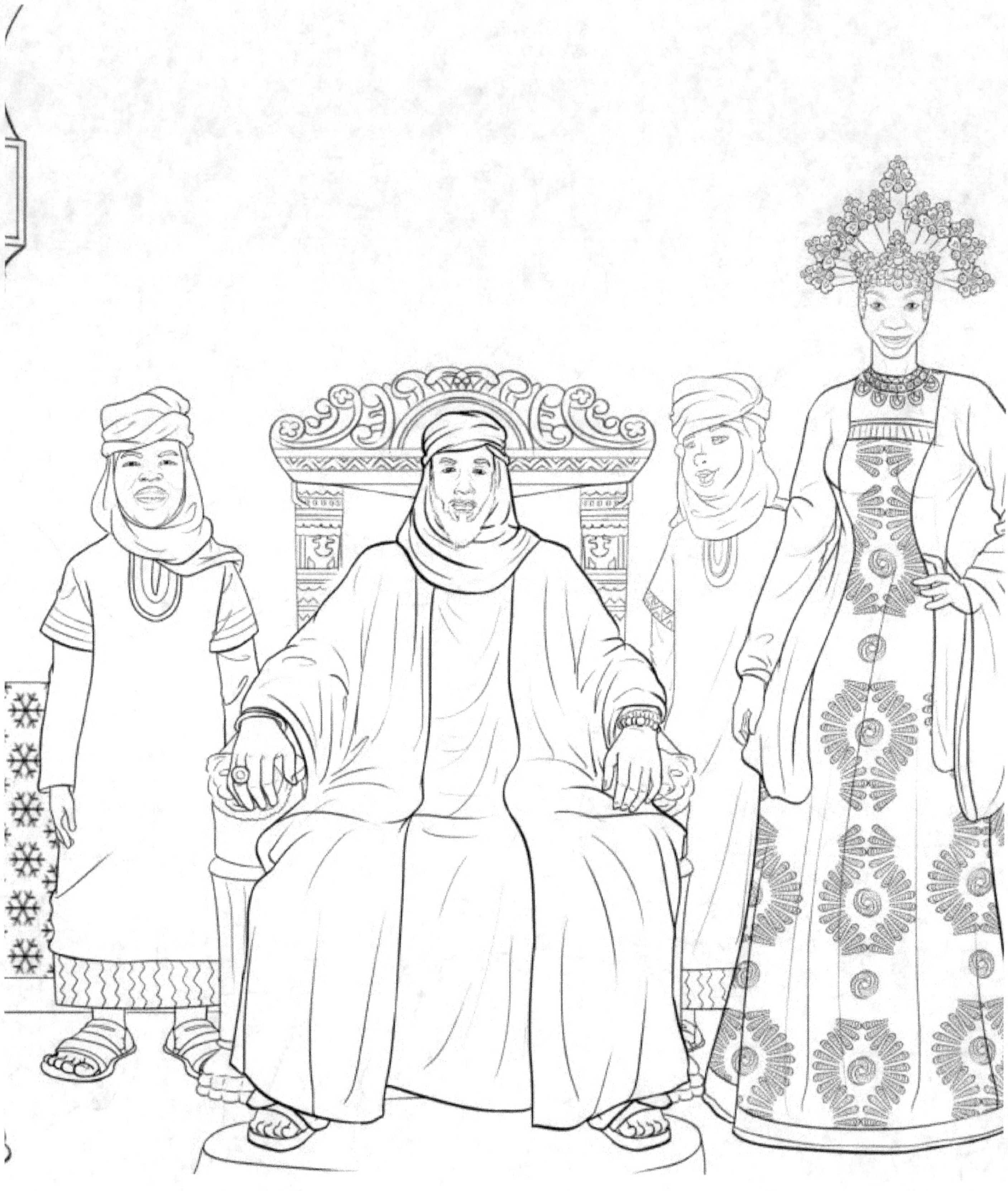

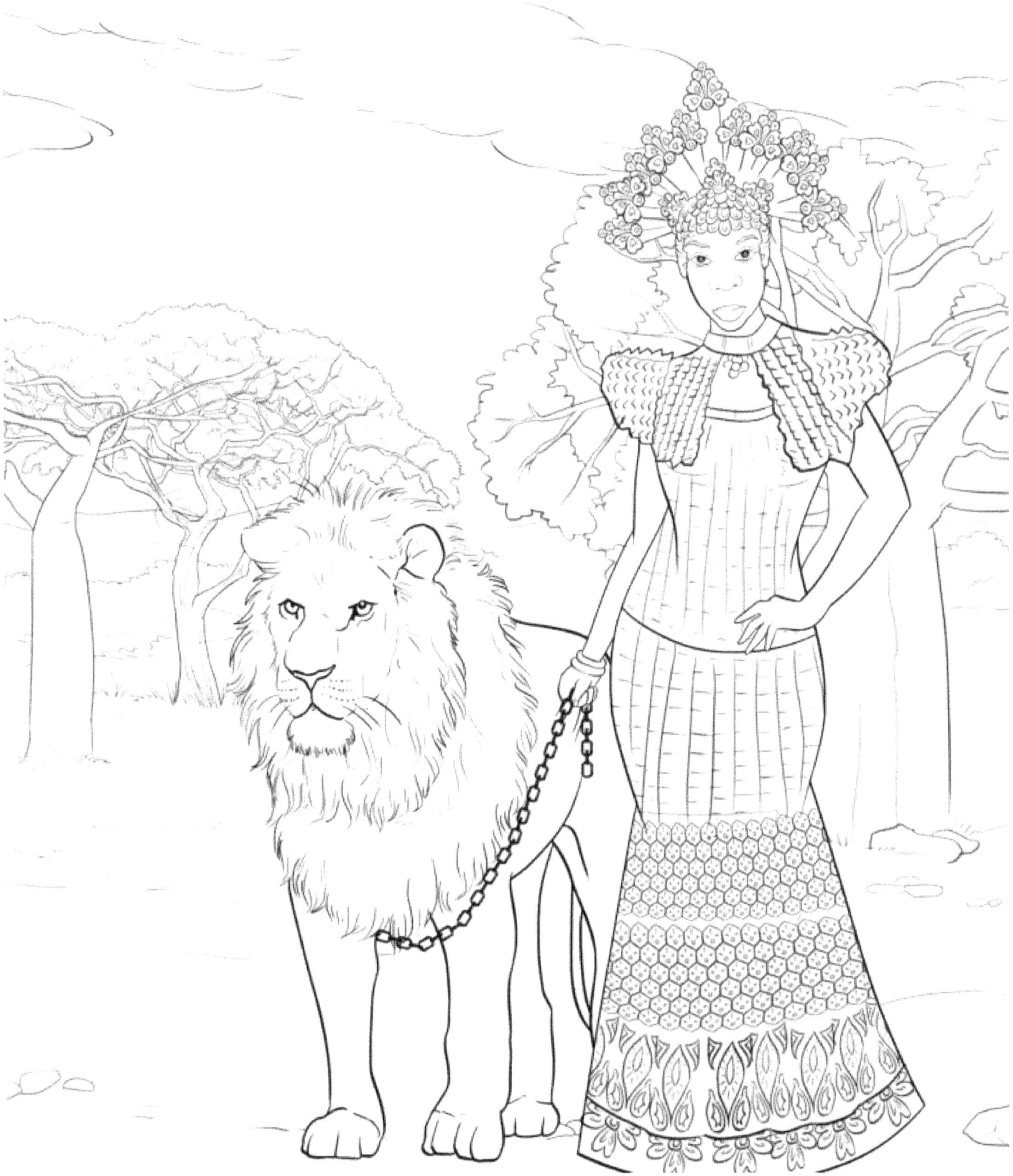

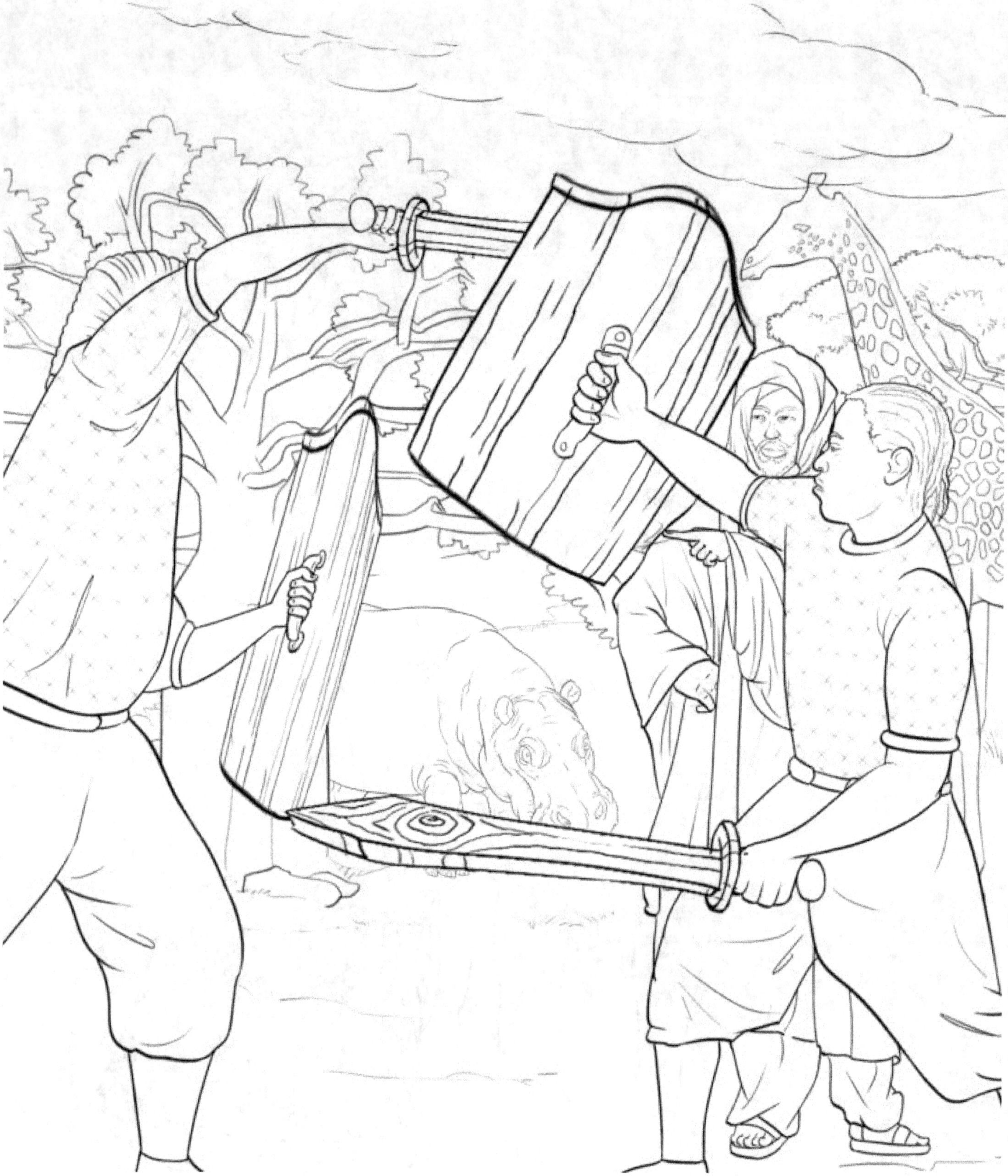

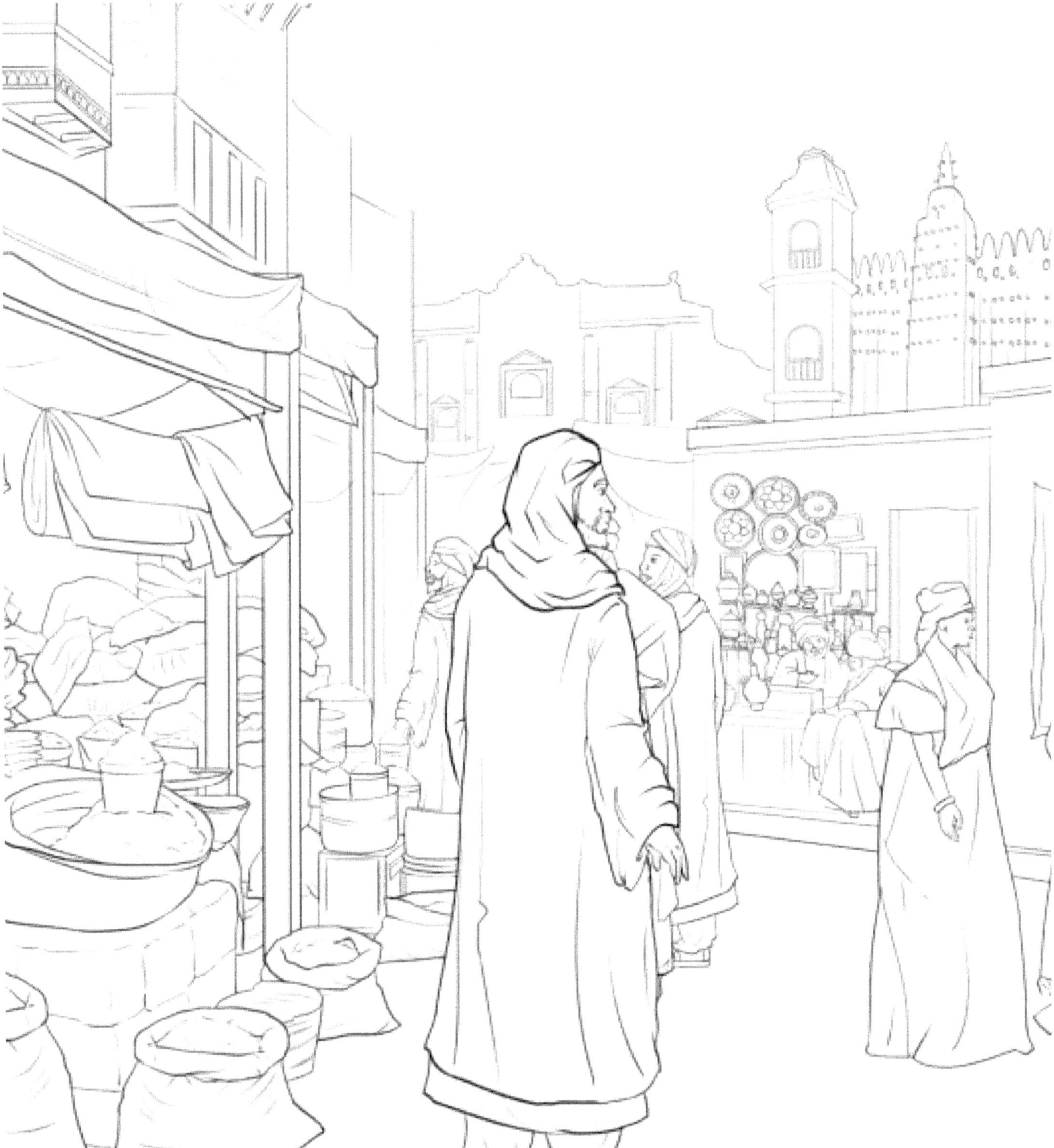

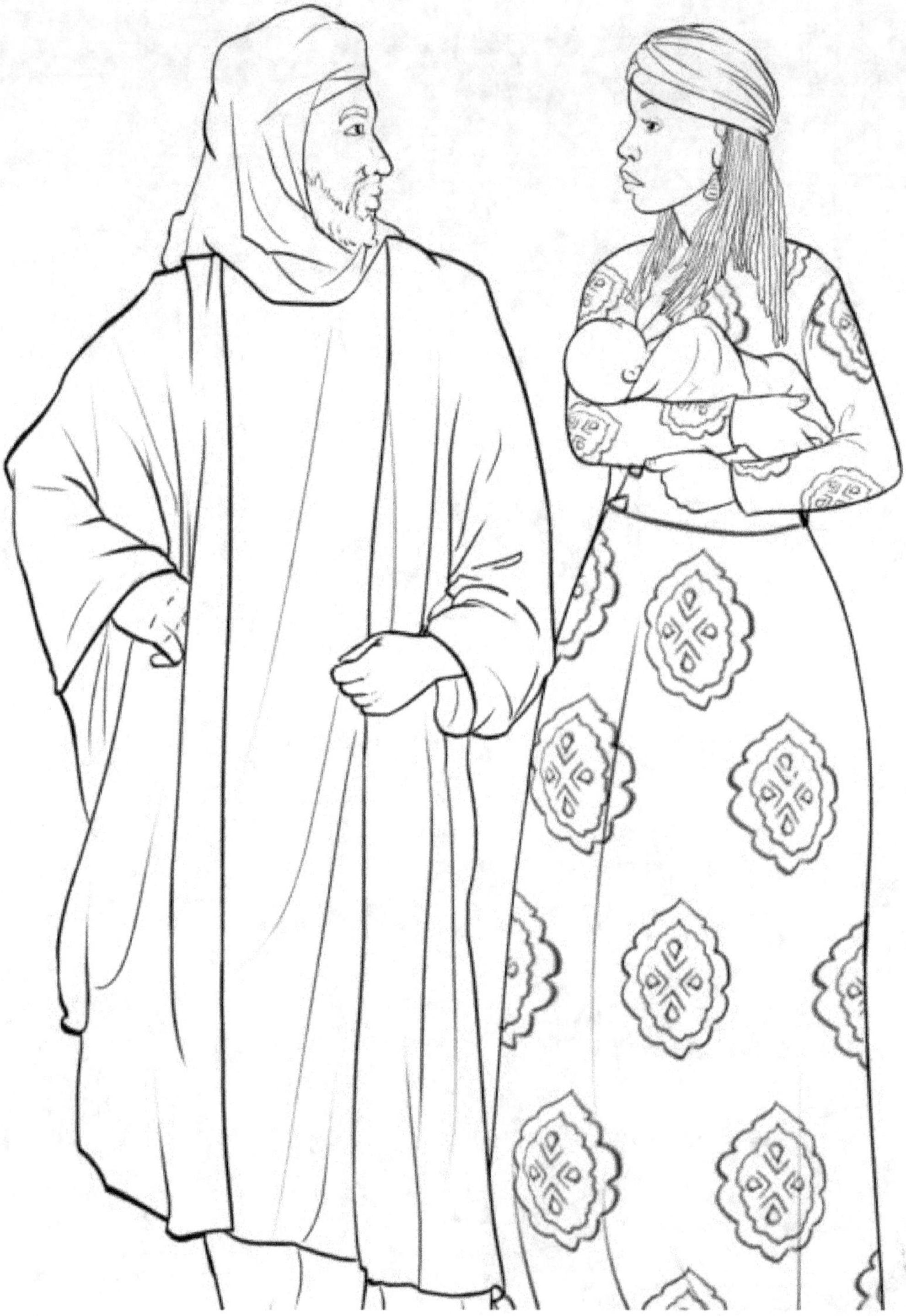

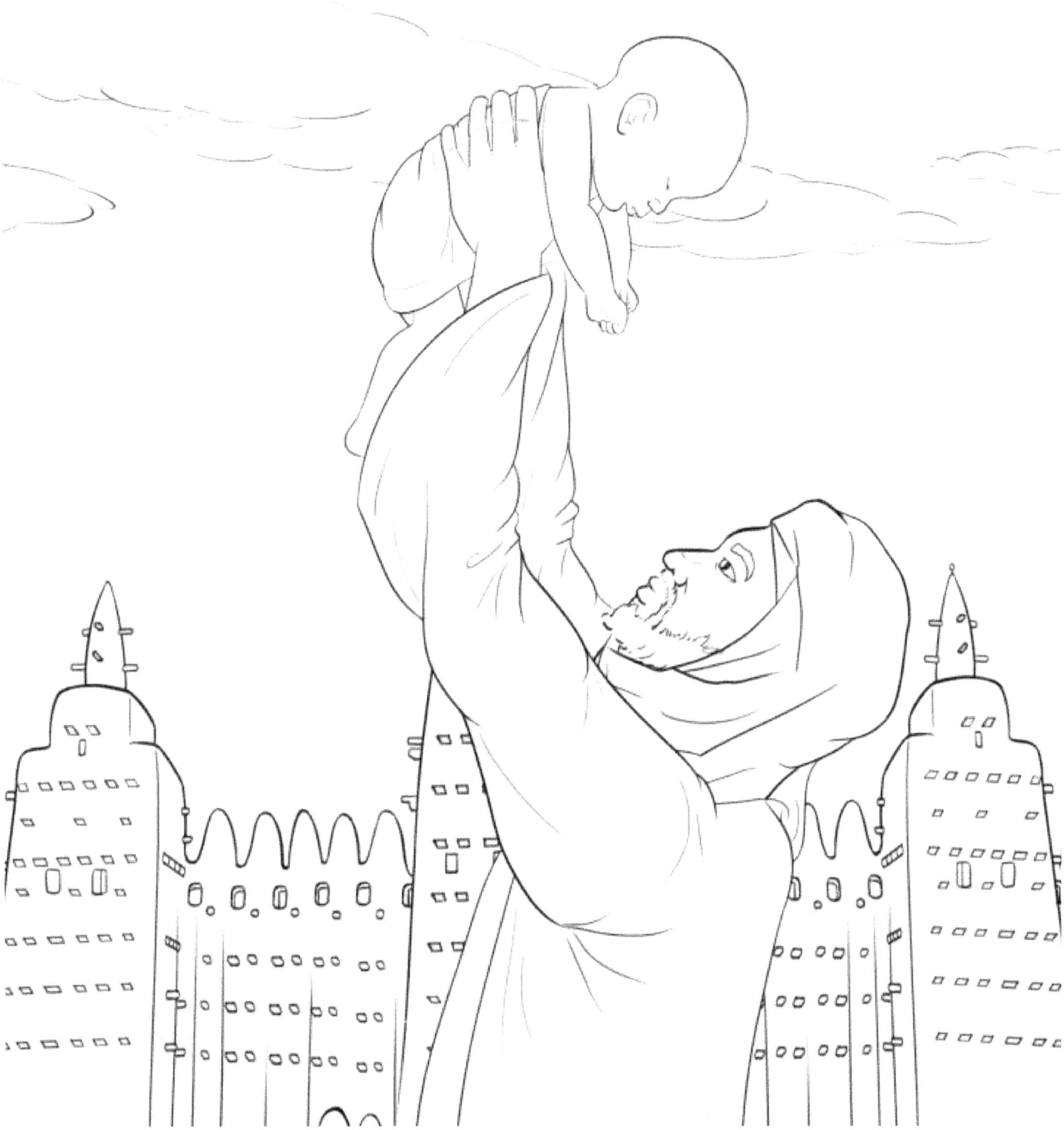

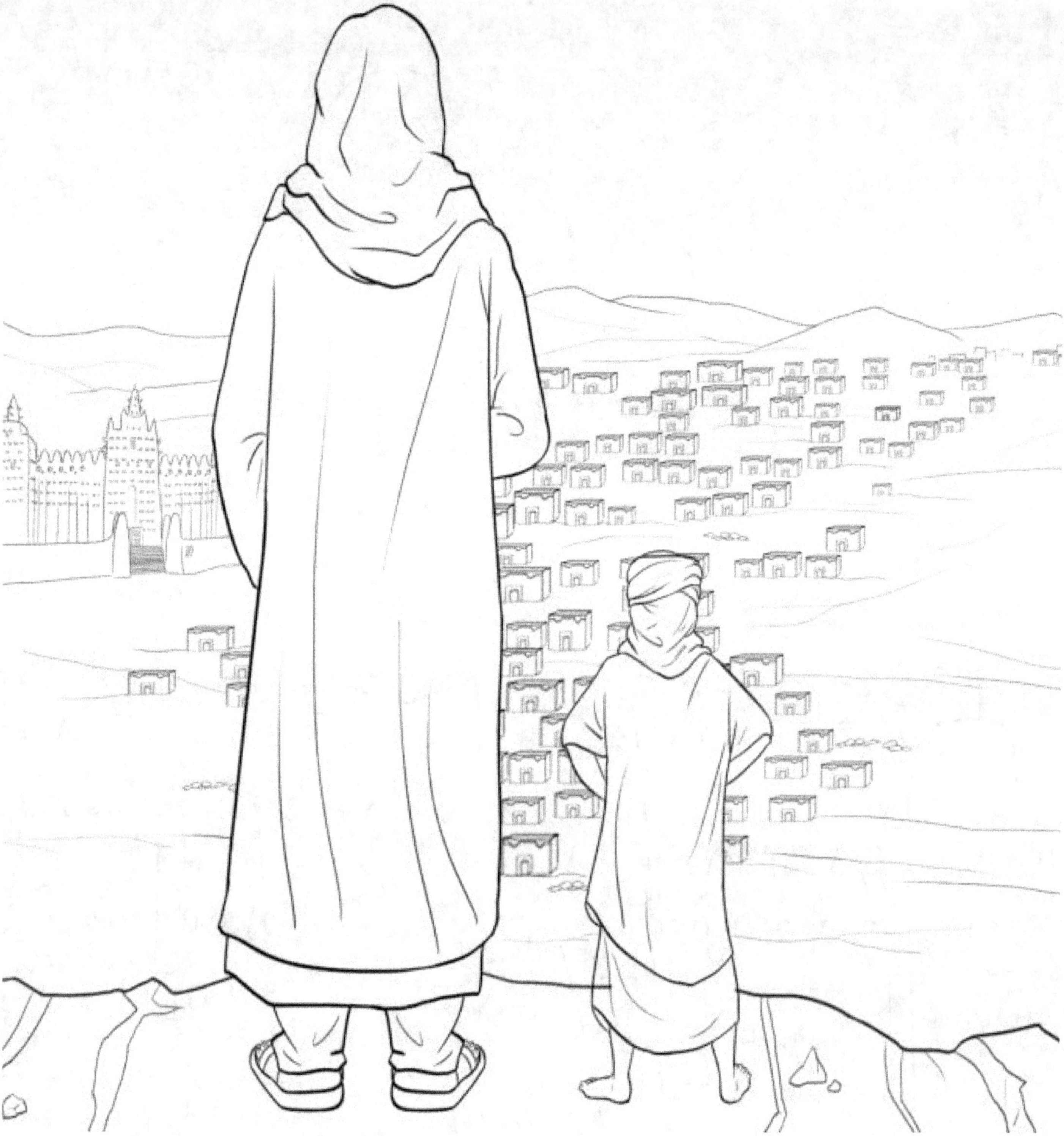

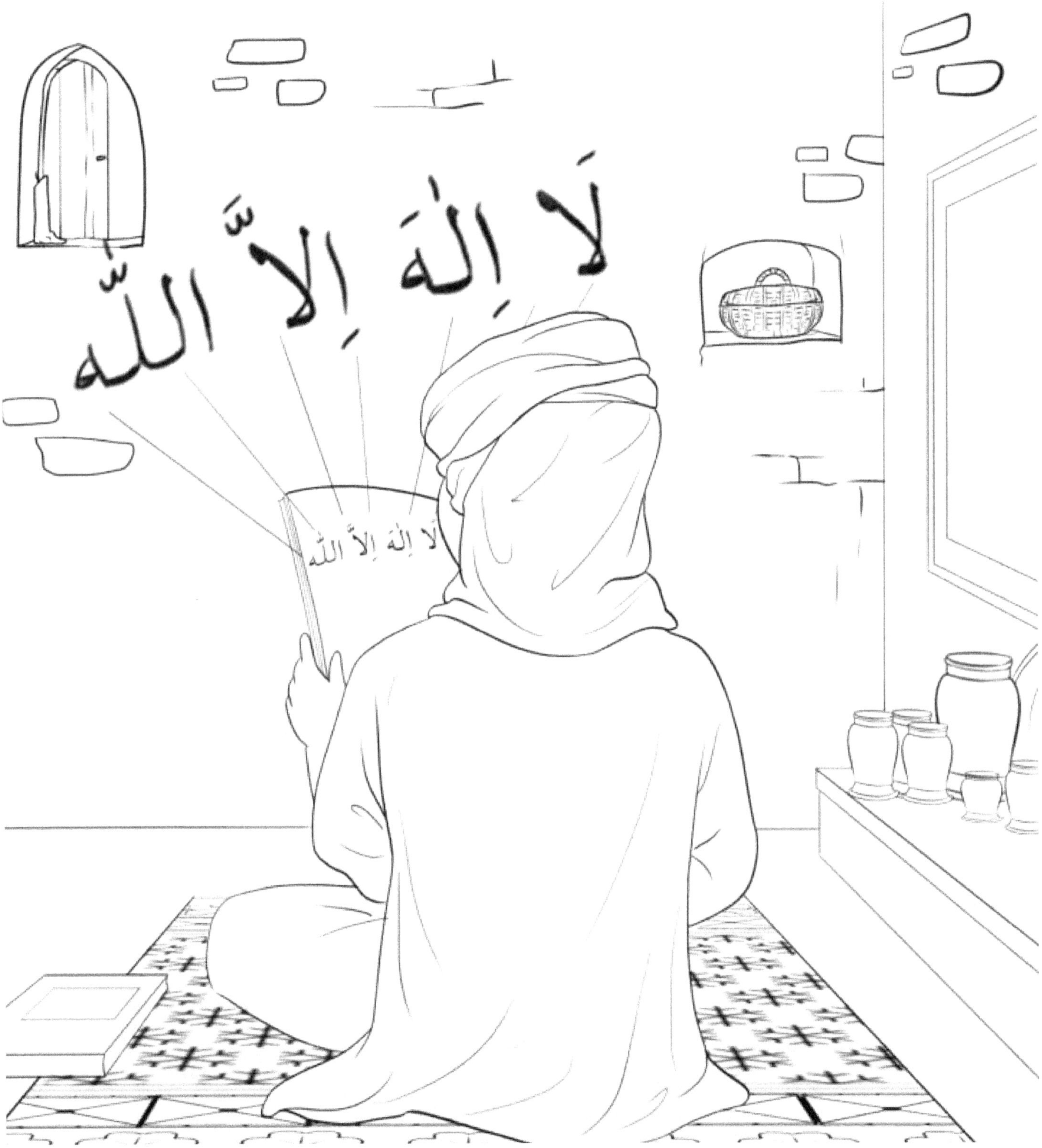

لَا إِلٰهَ إِلَّا اللّٰه
لا إله إلاَّ اللّه

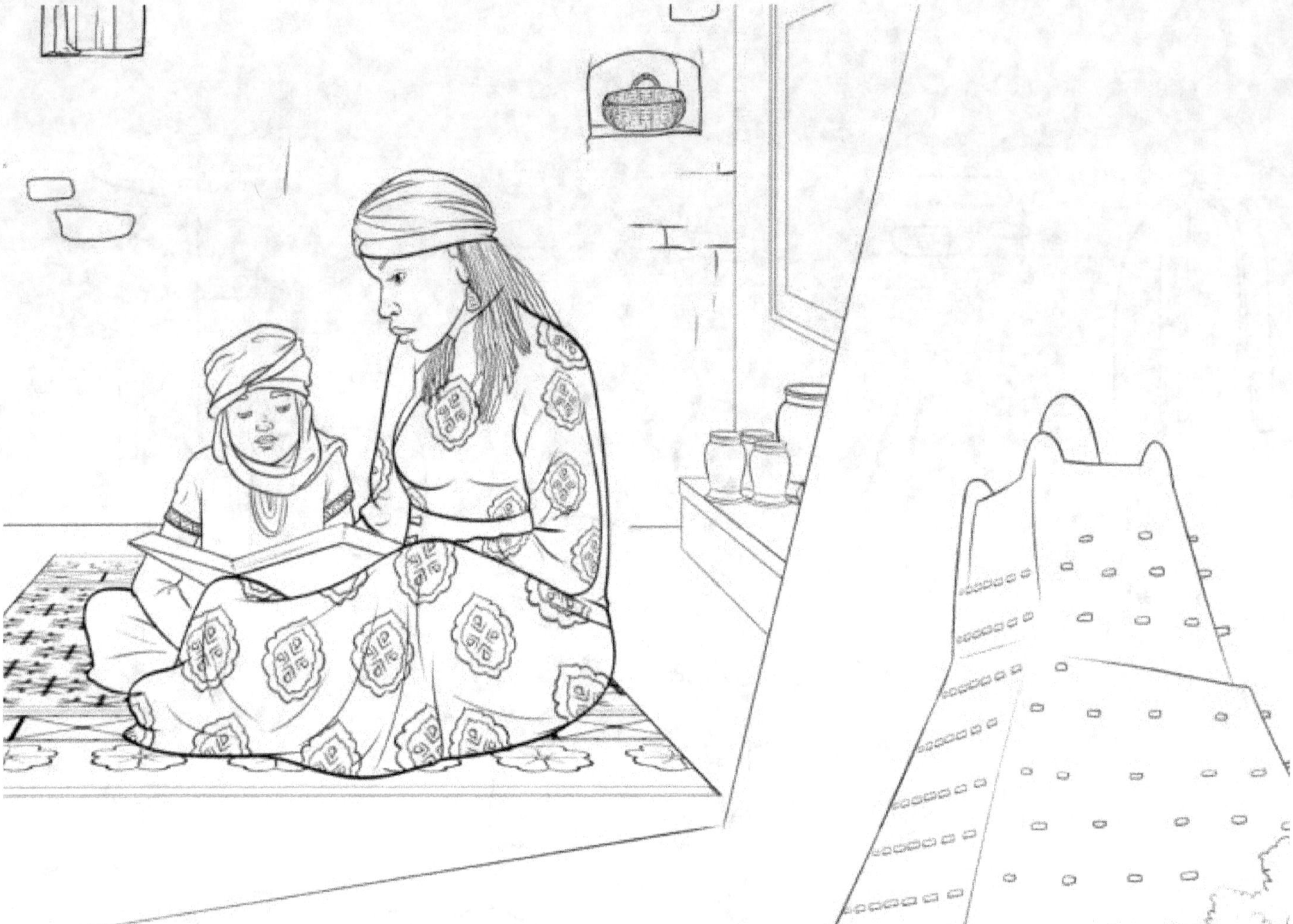

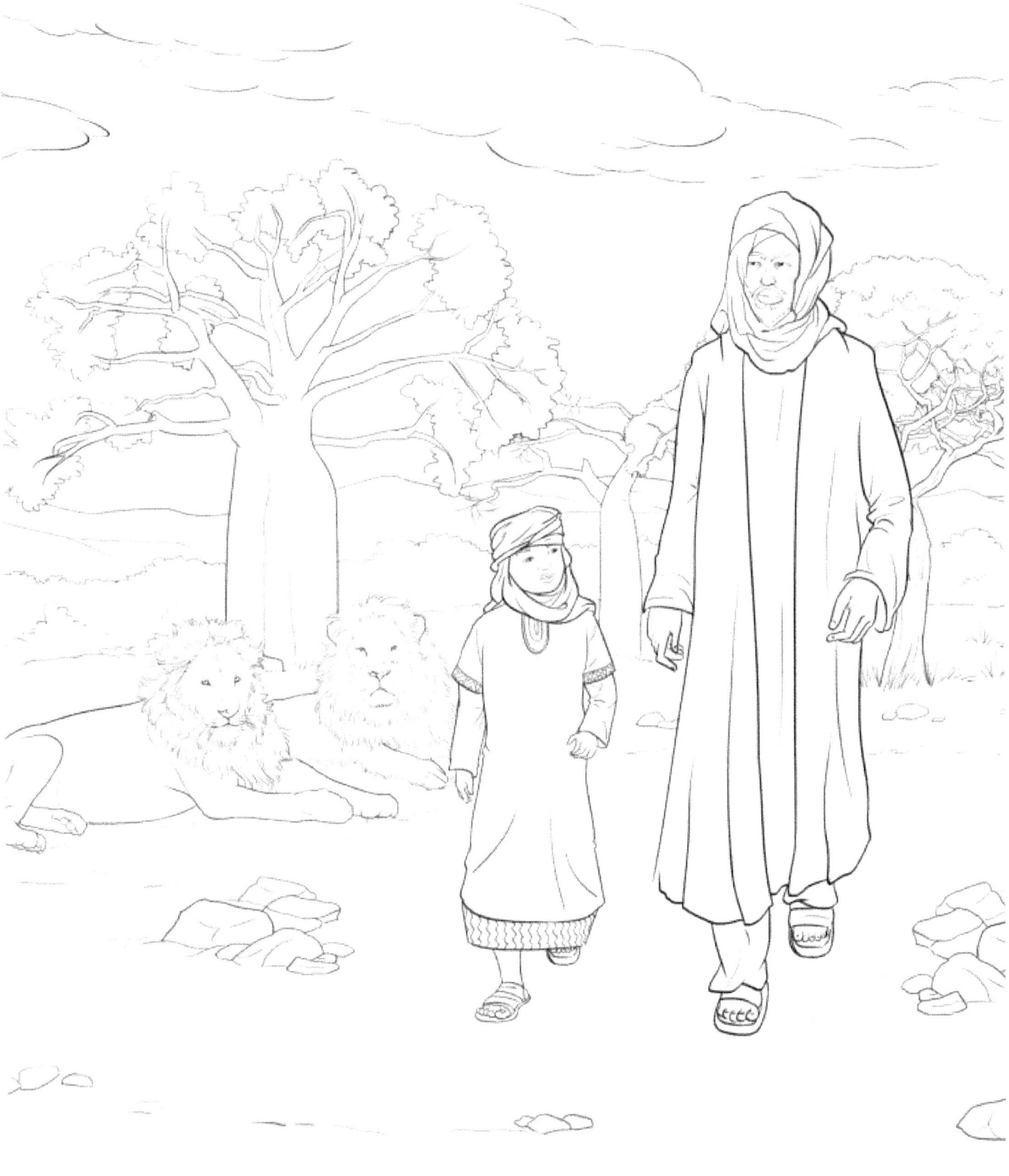

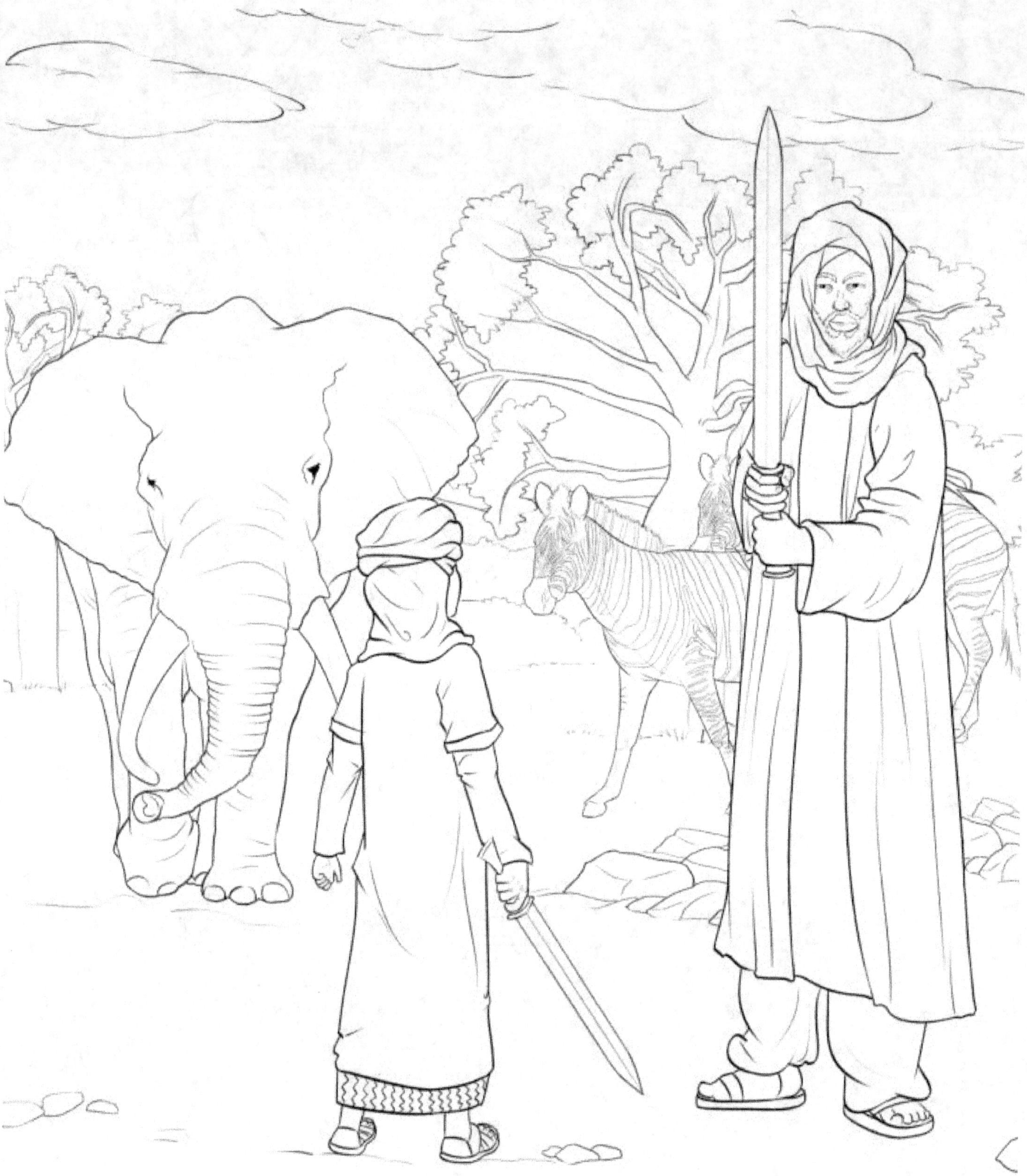

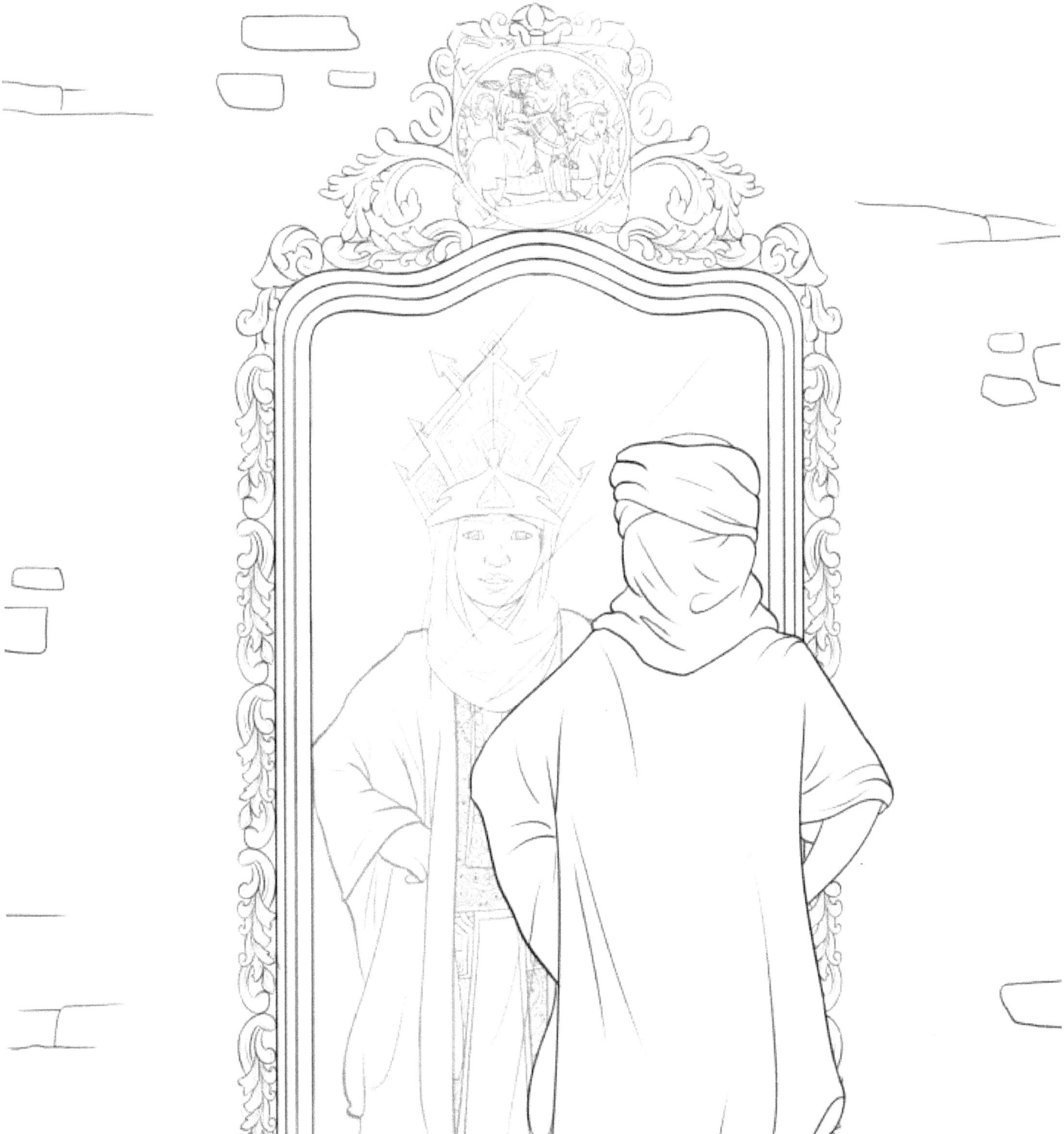

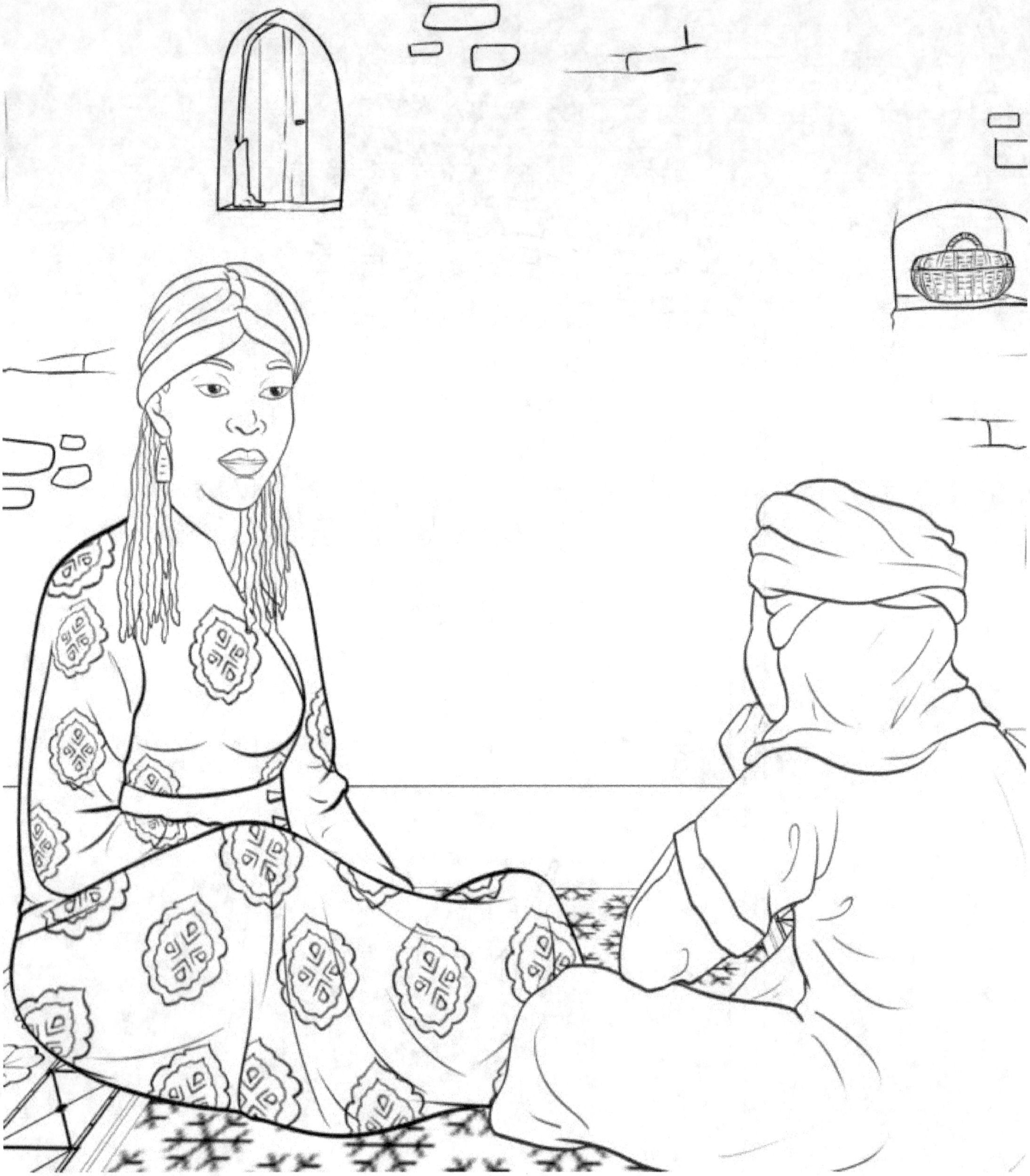

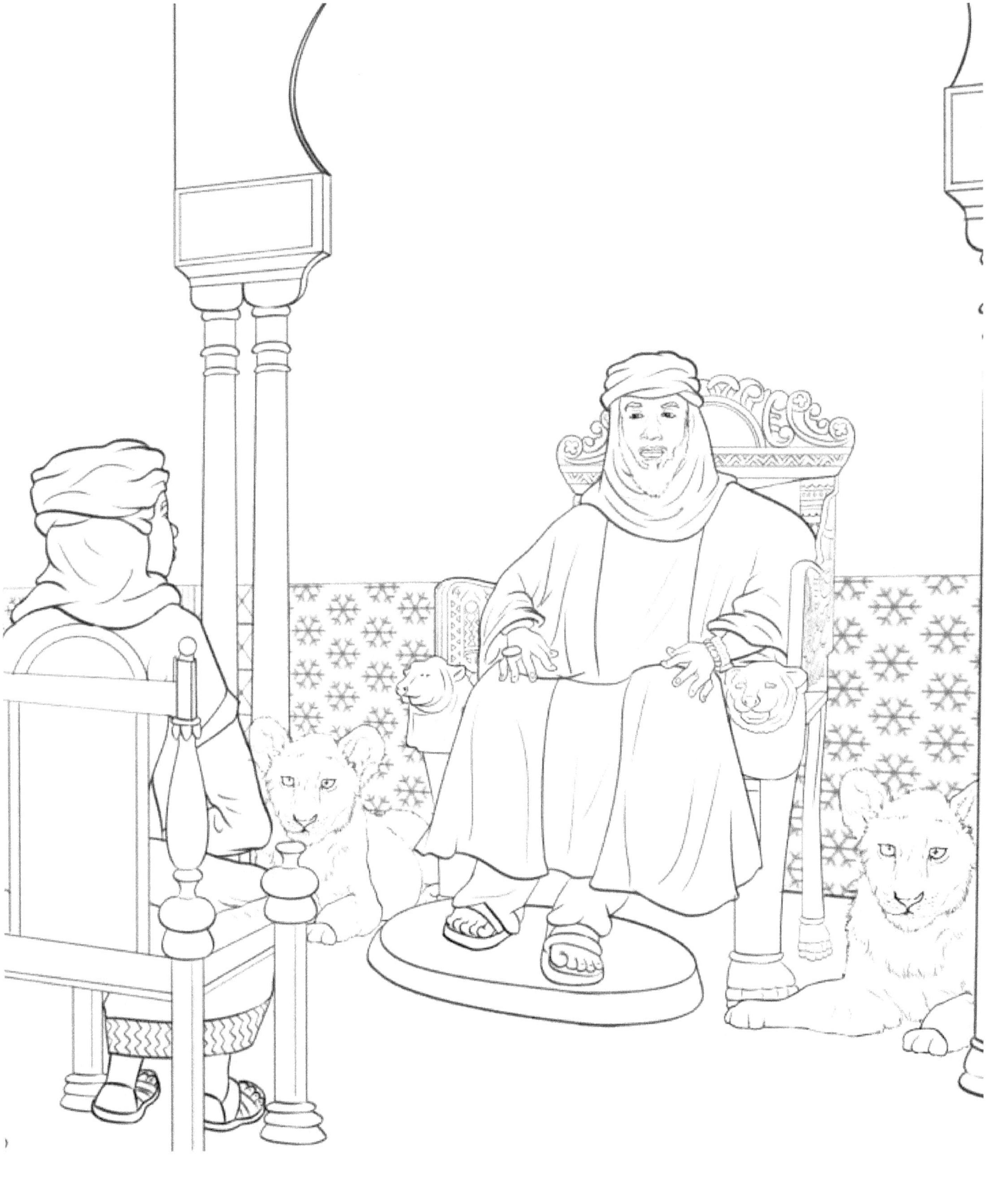

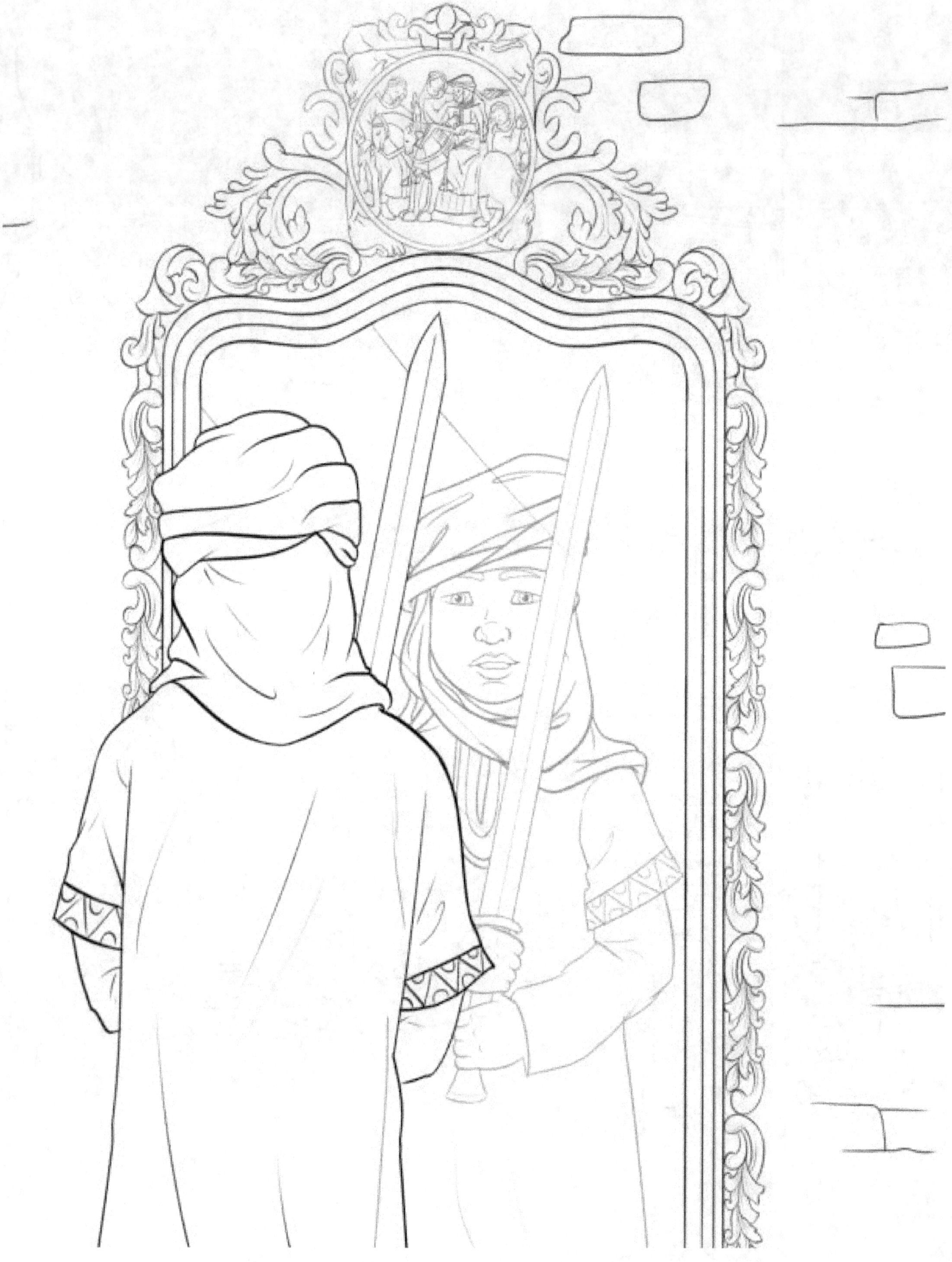

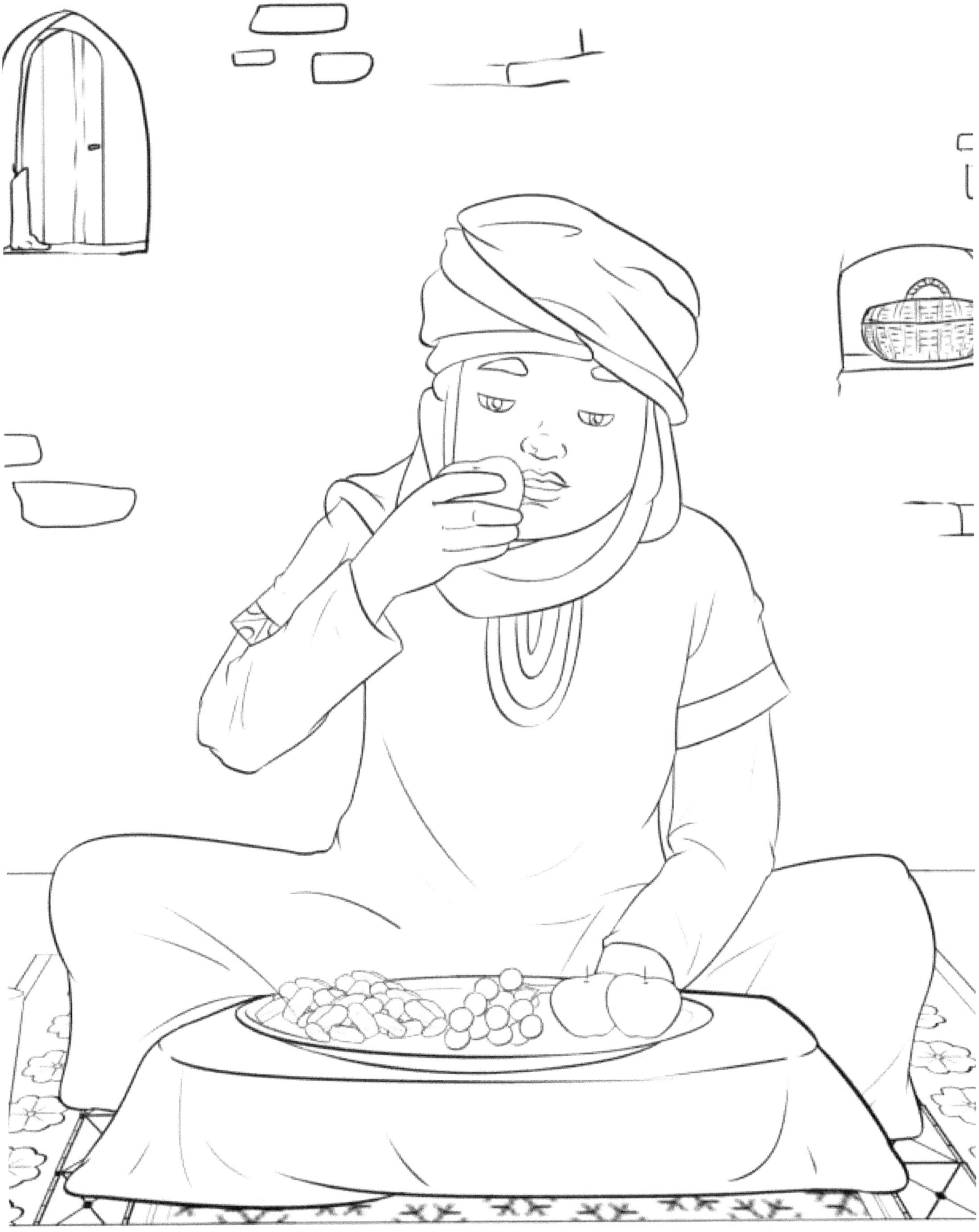

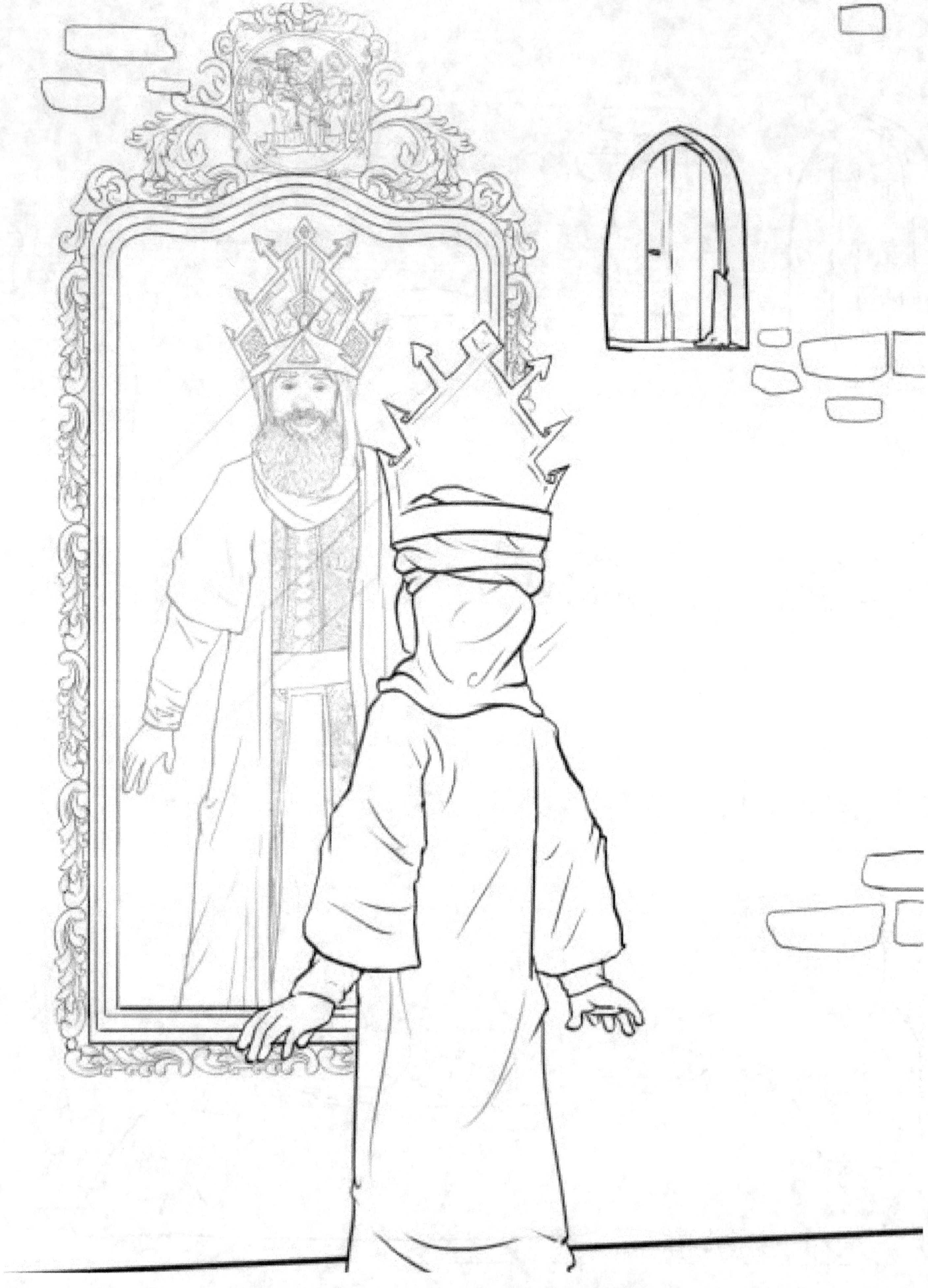

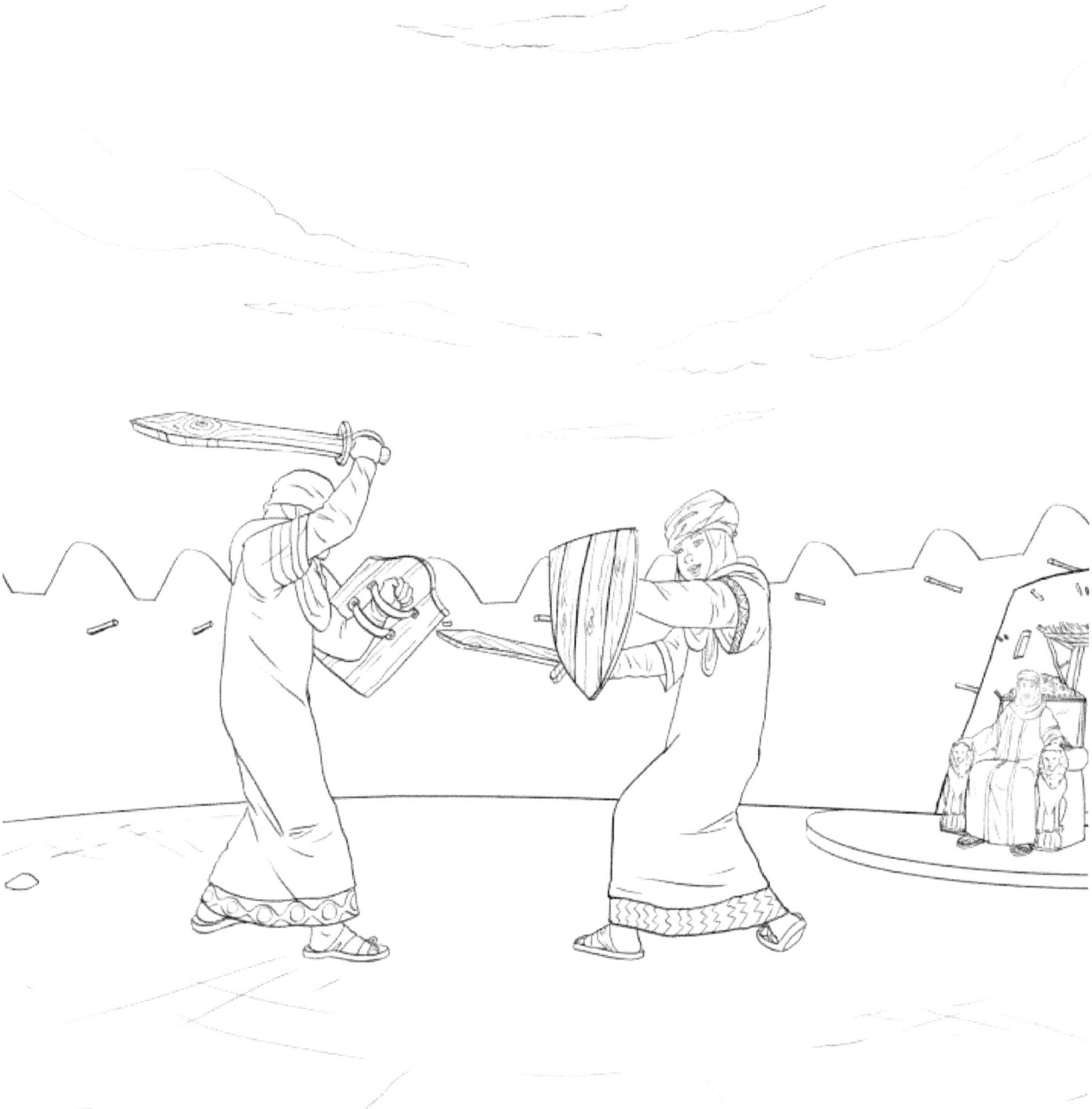

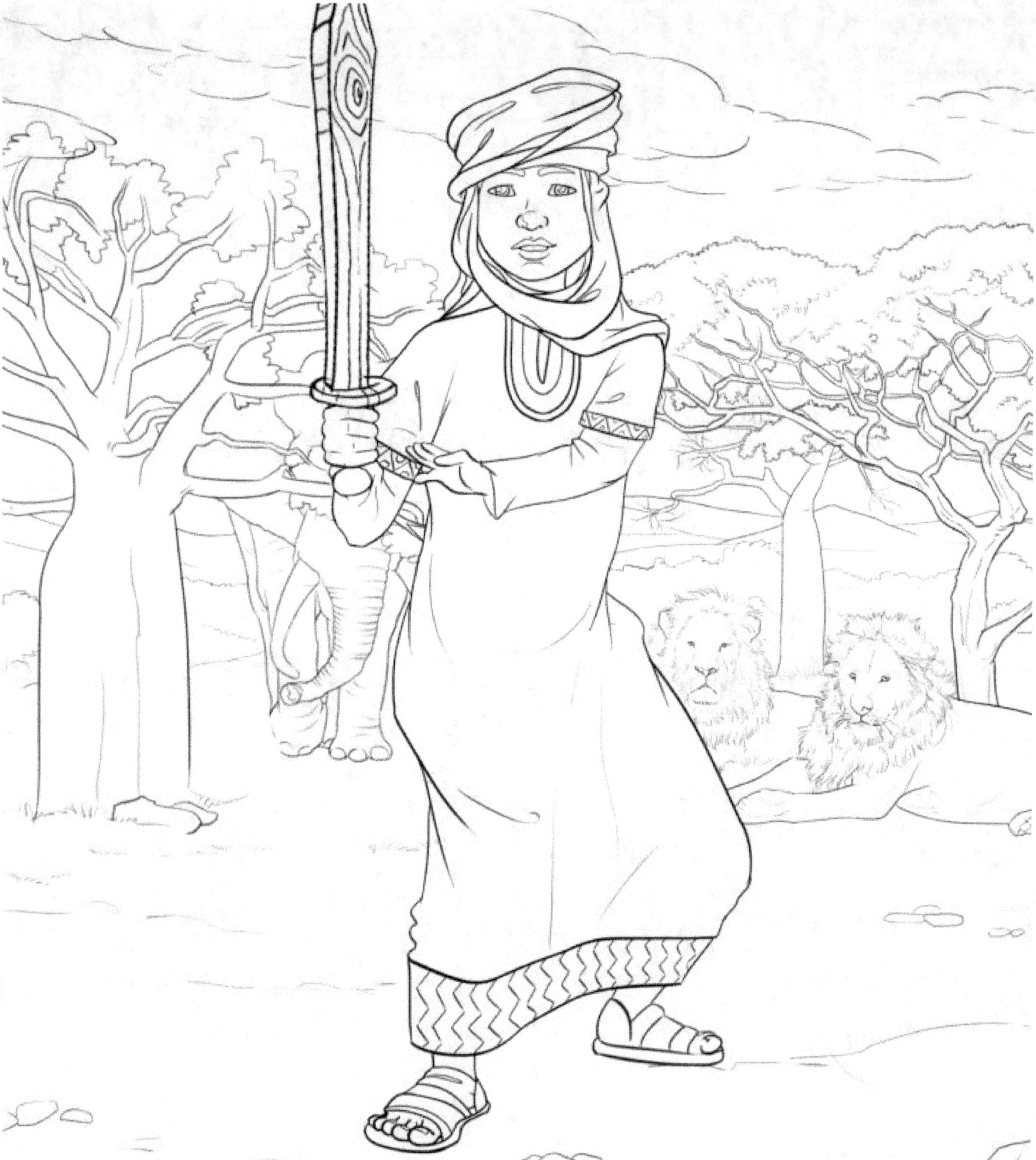

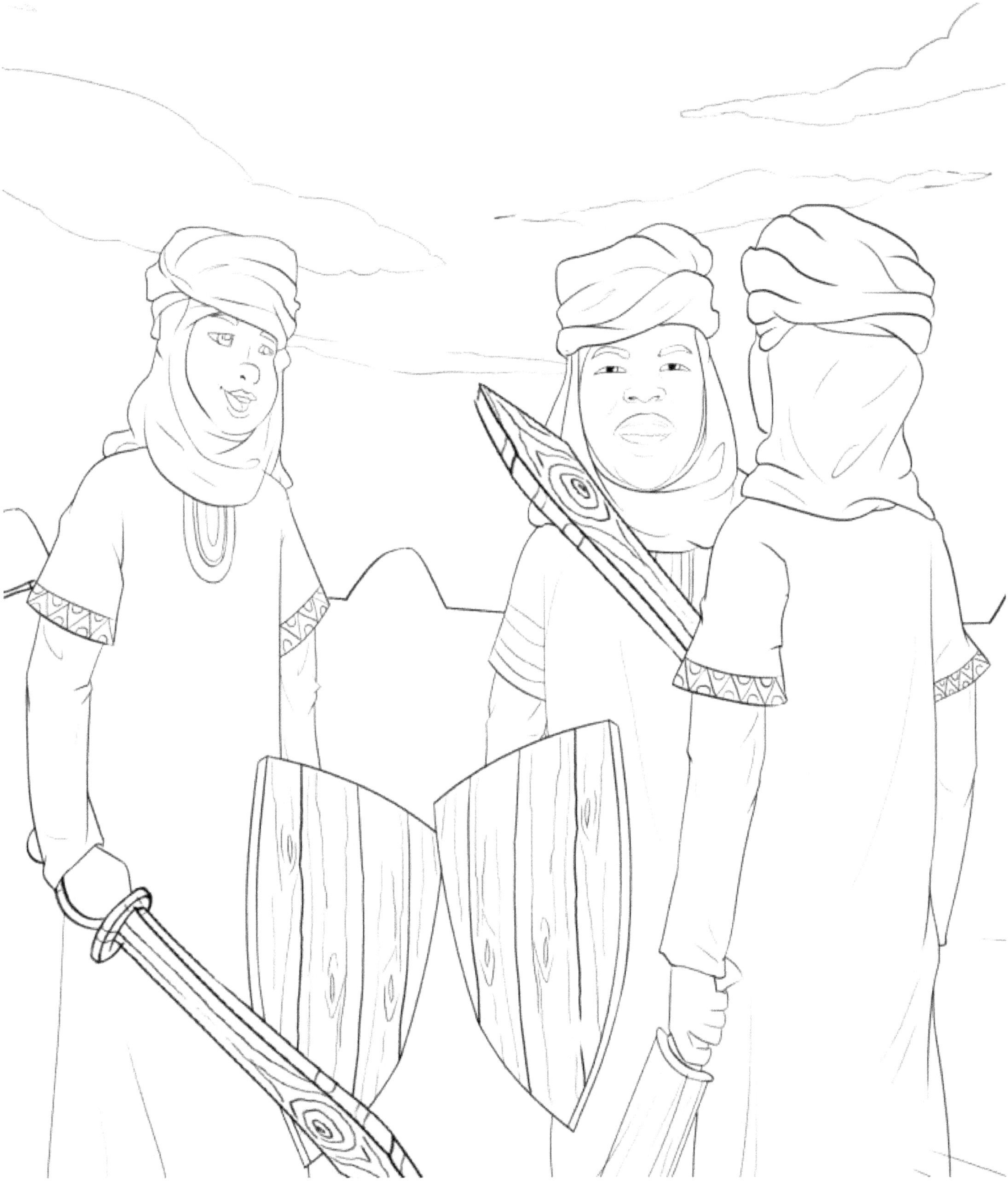

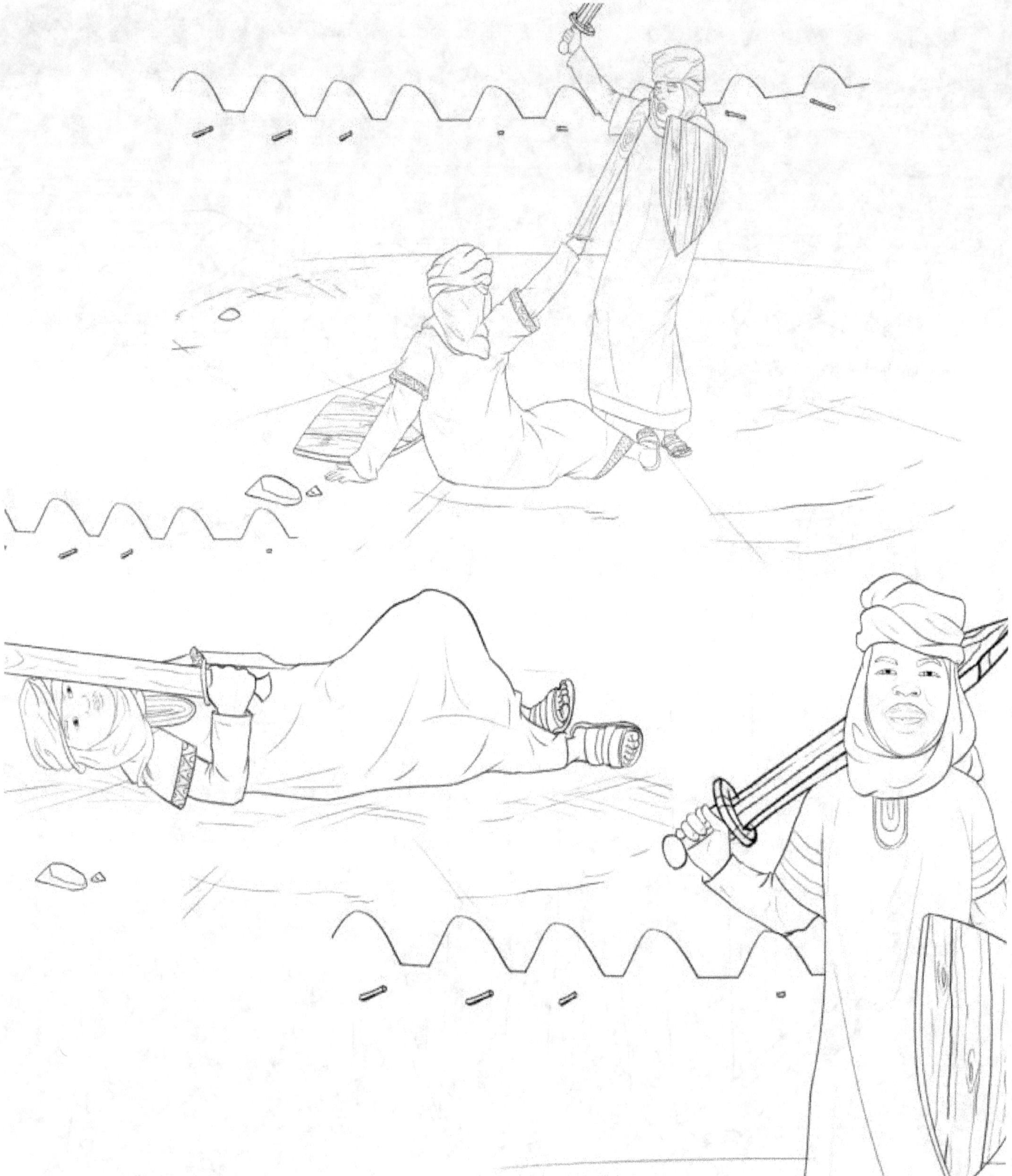

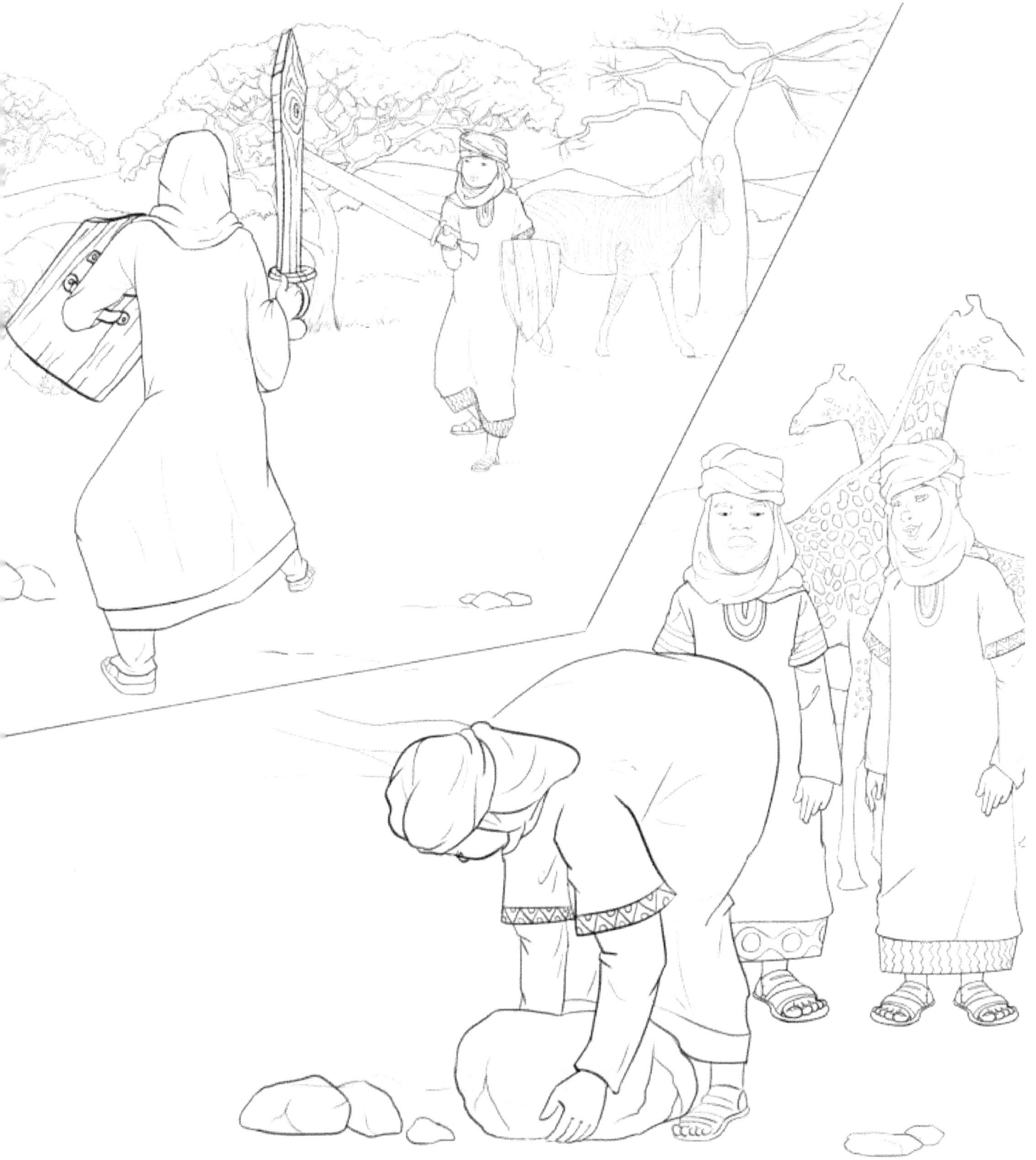

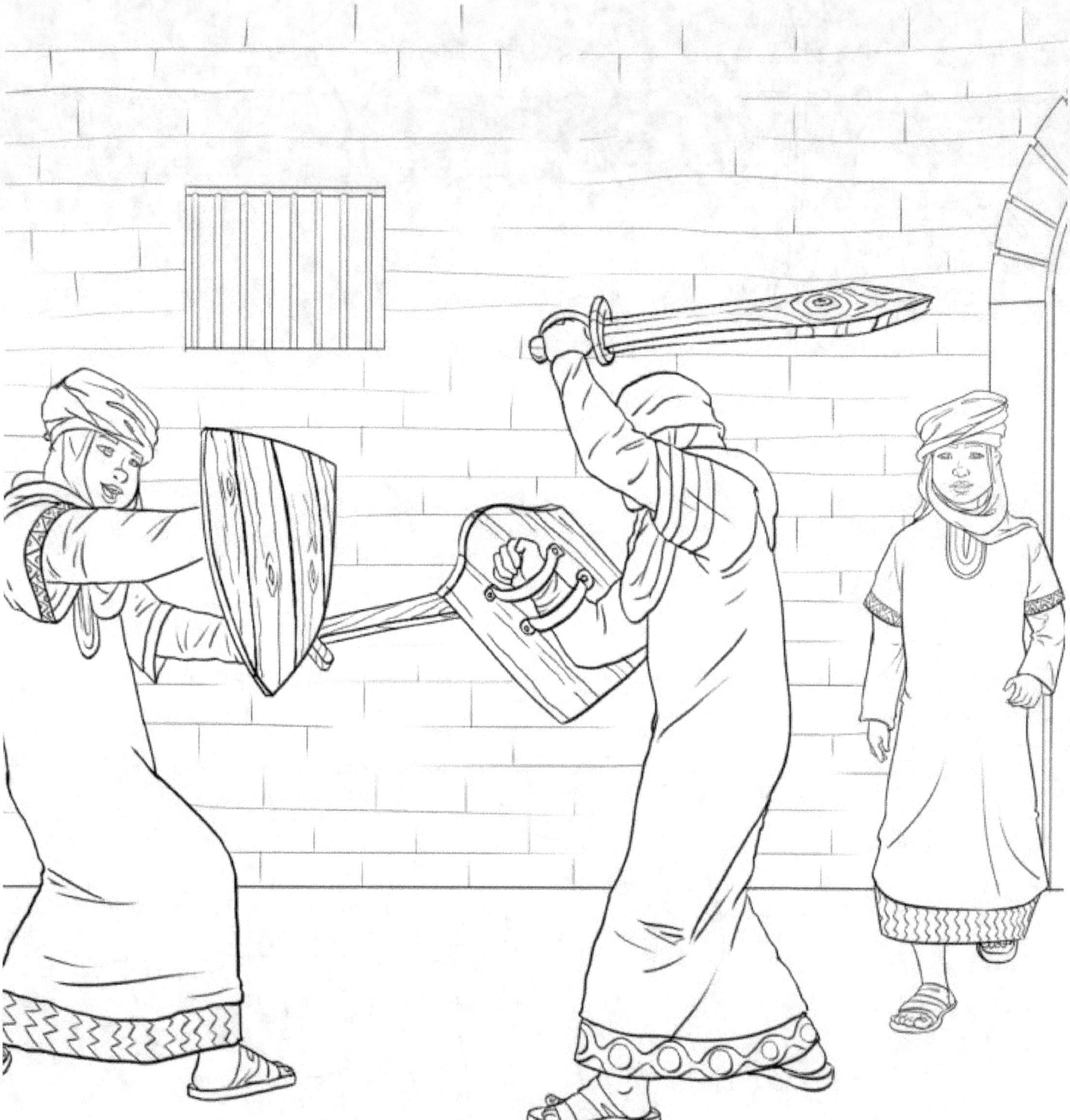

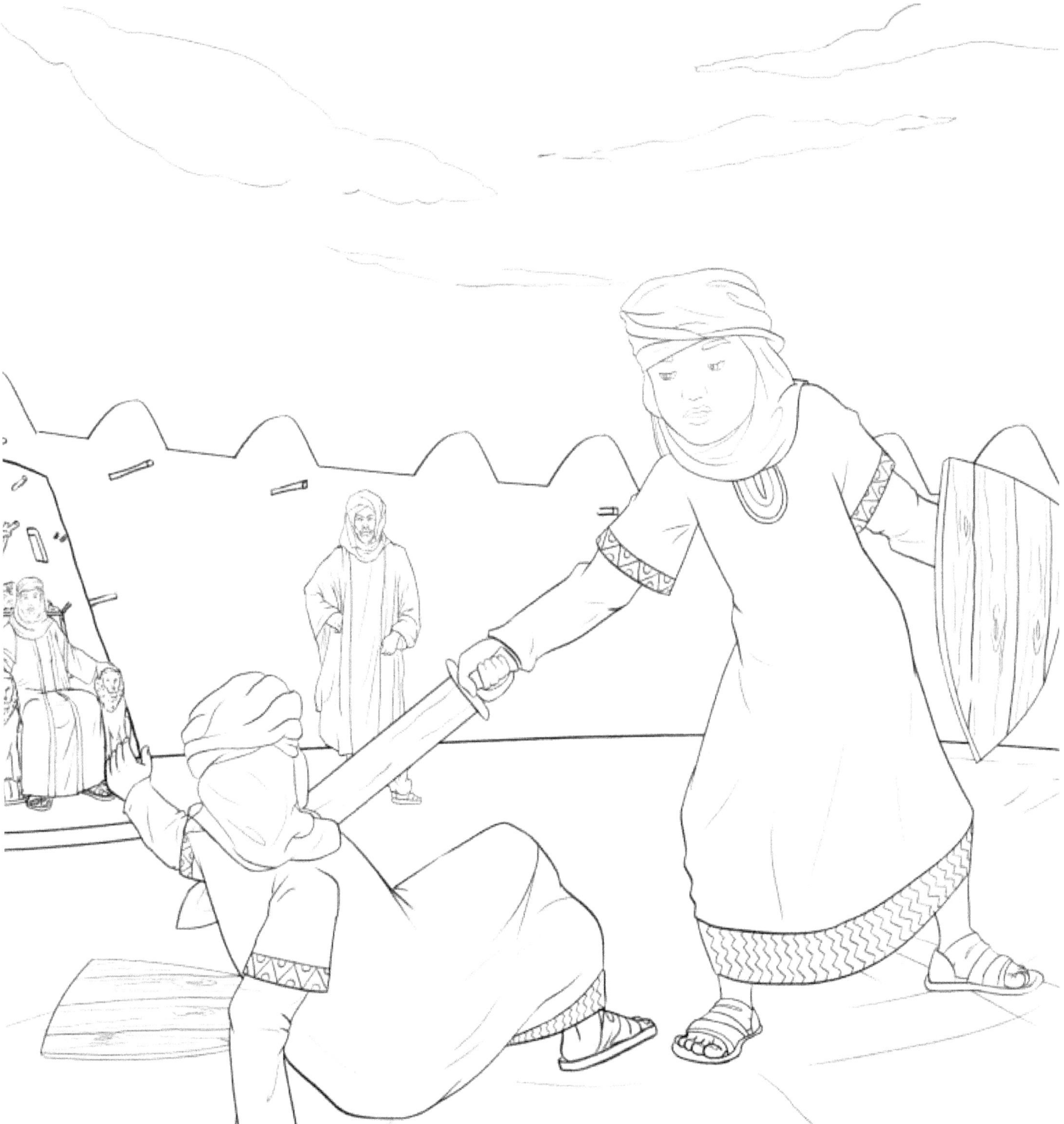

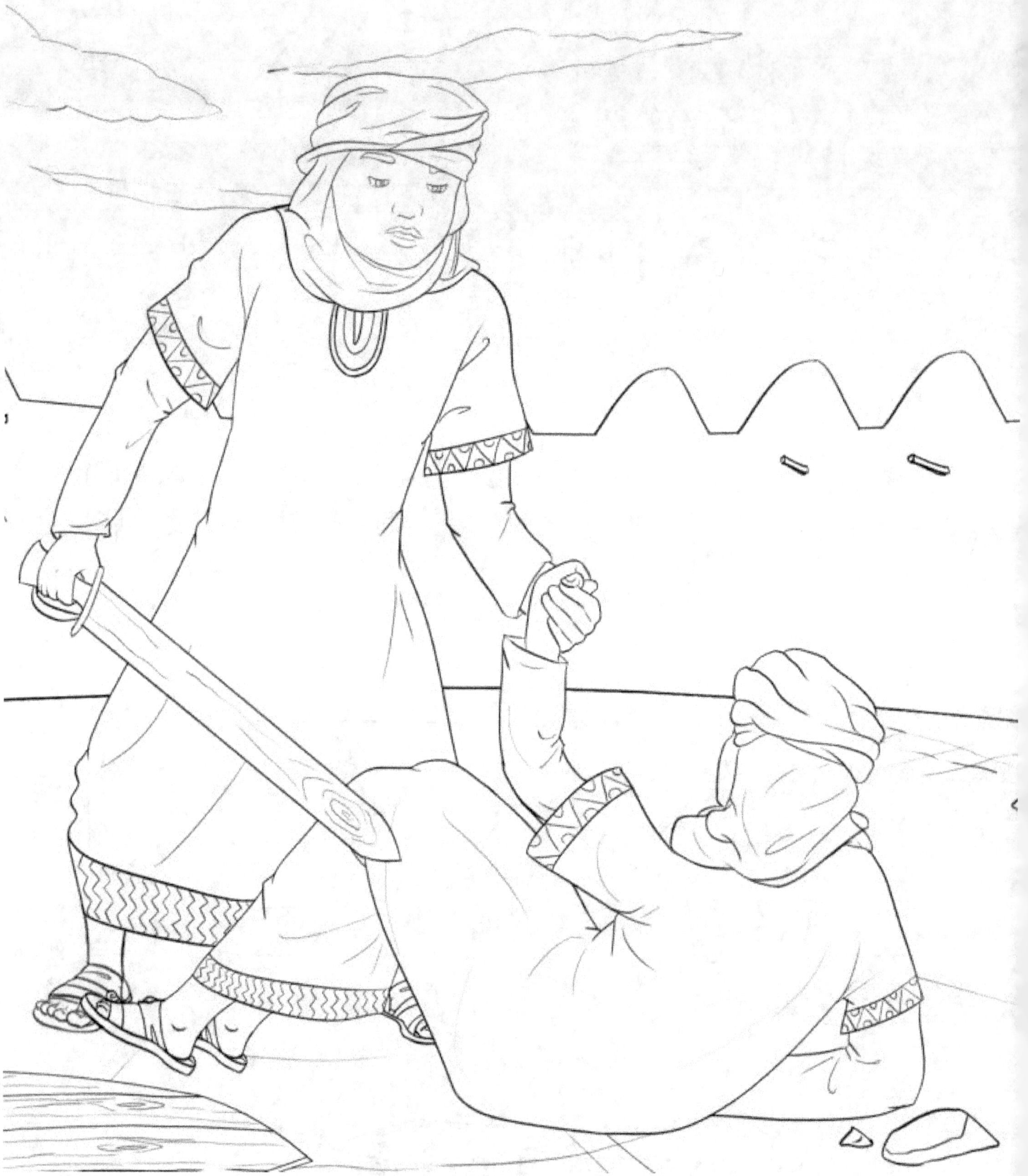

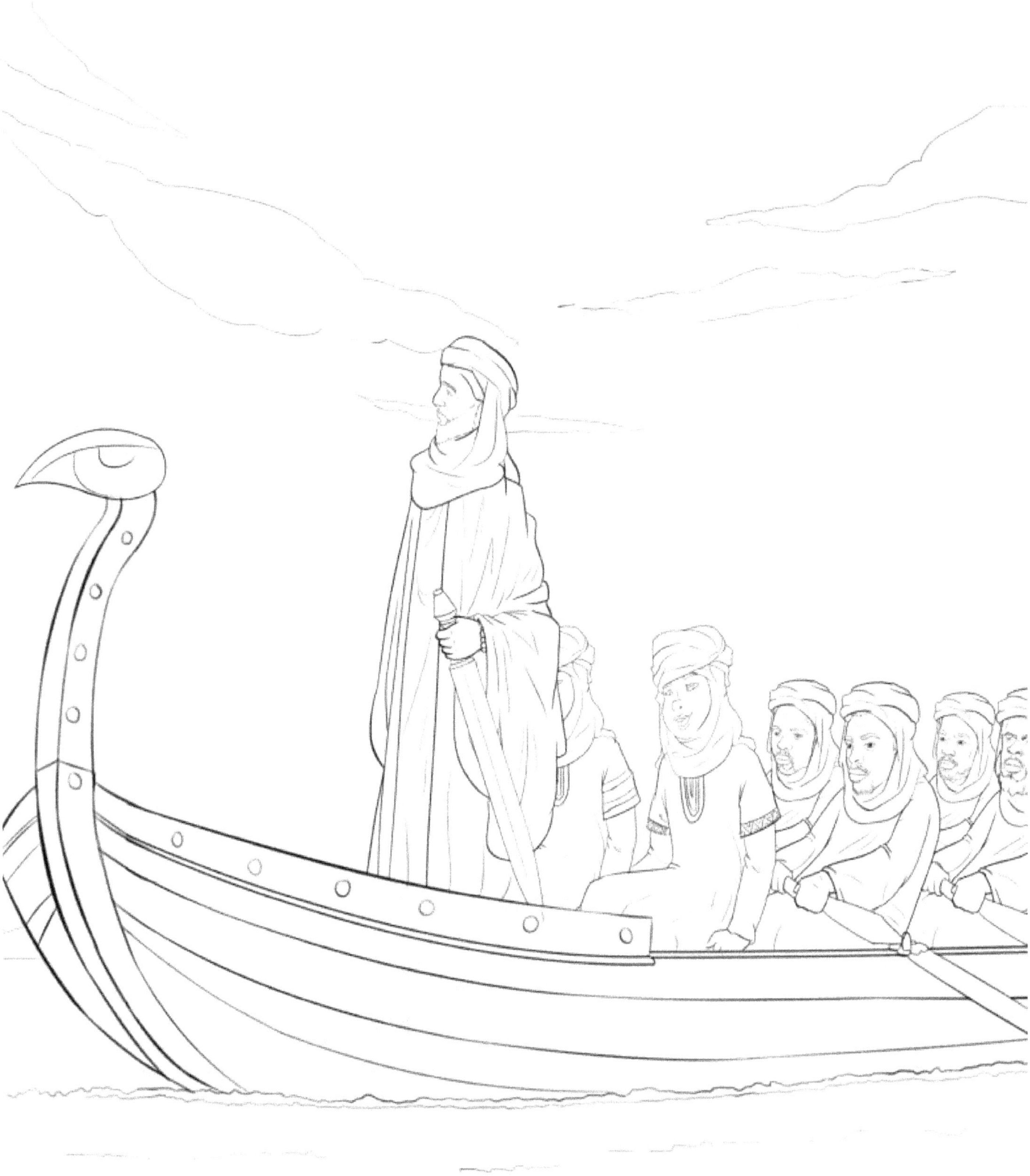

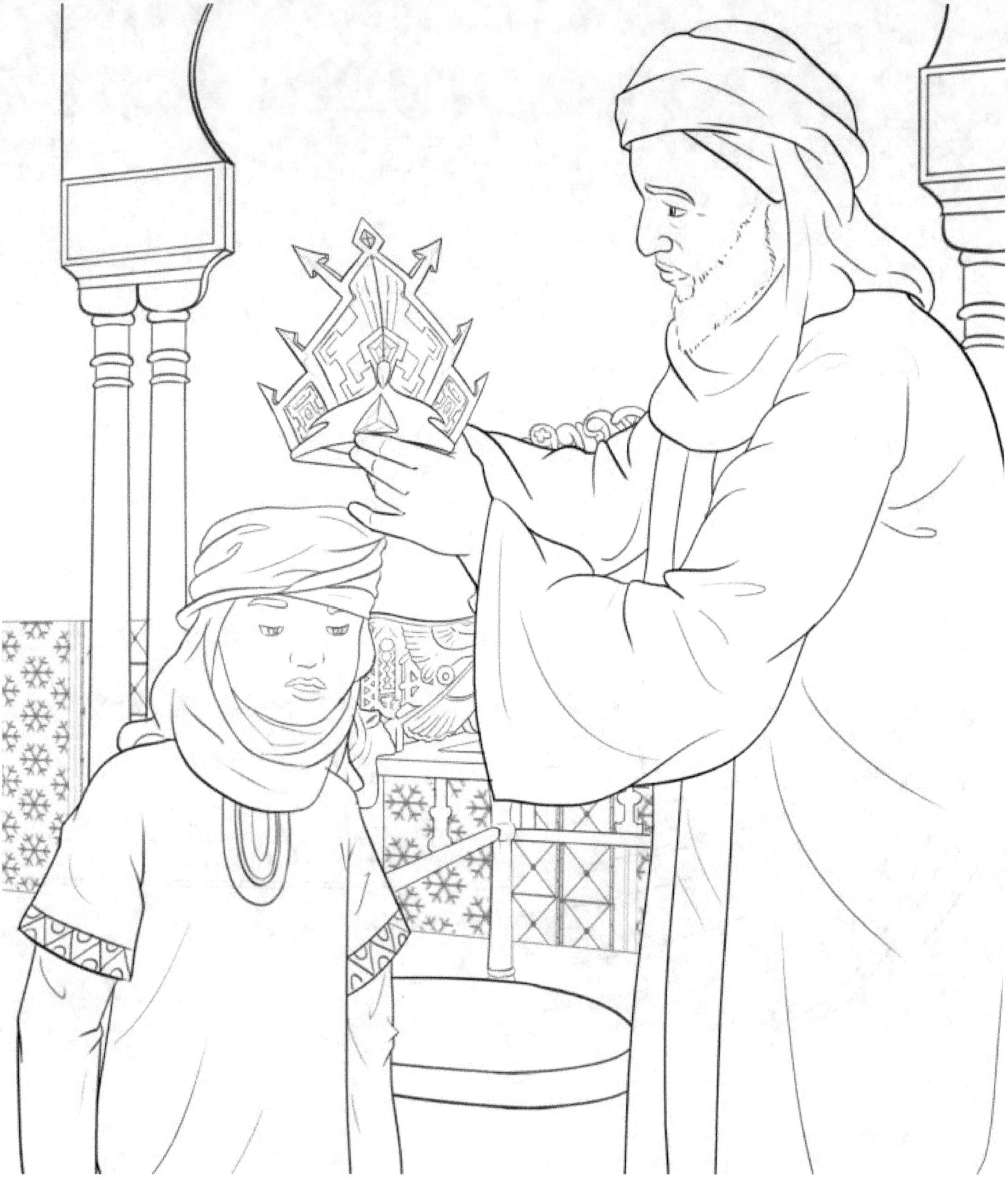

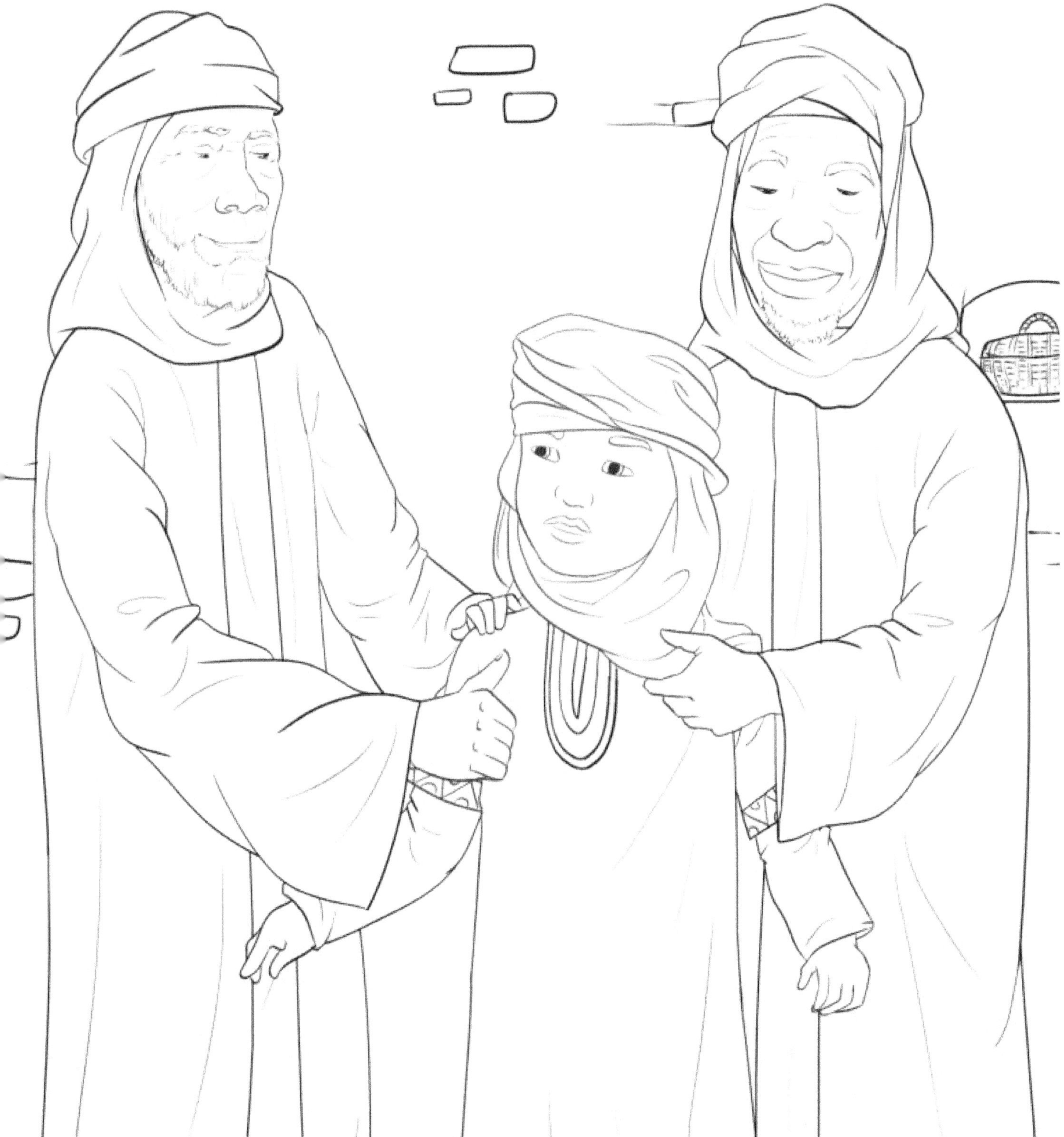

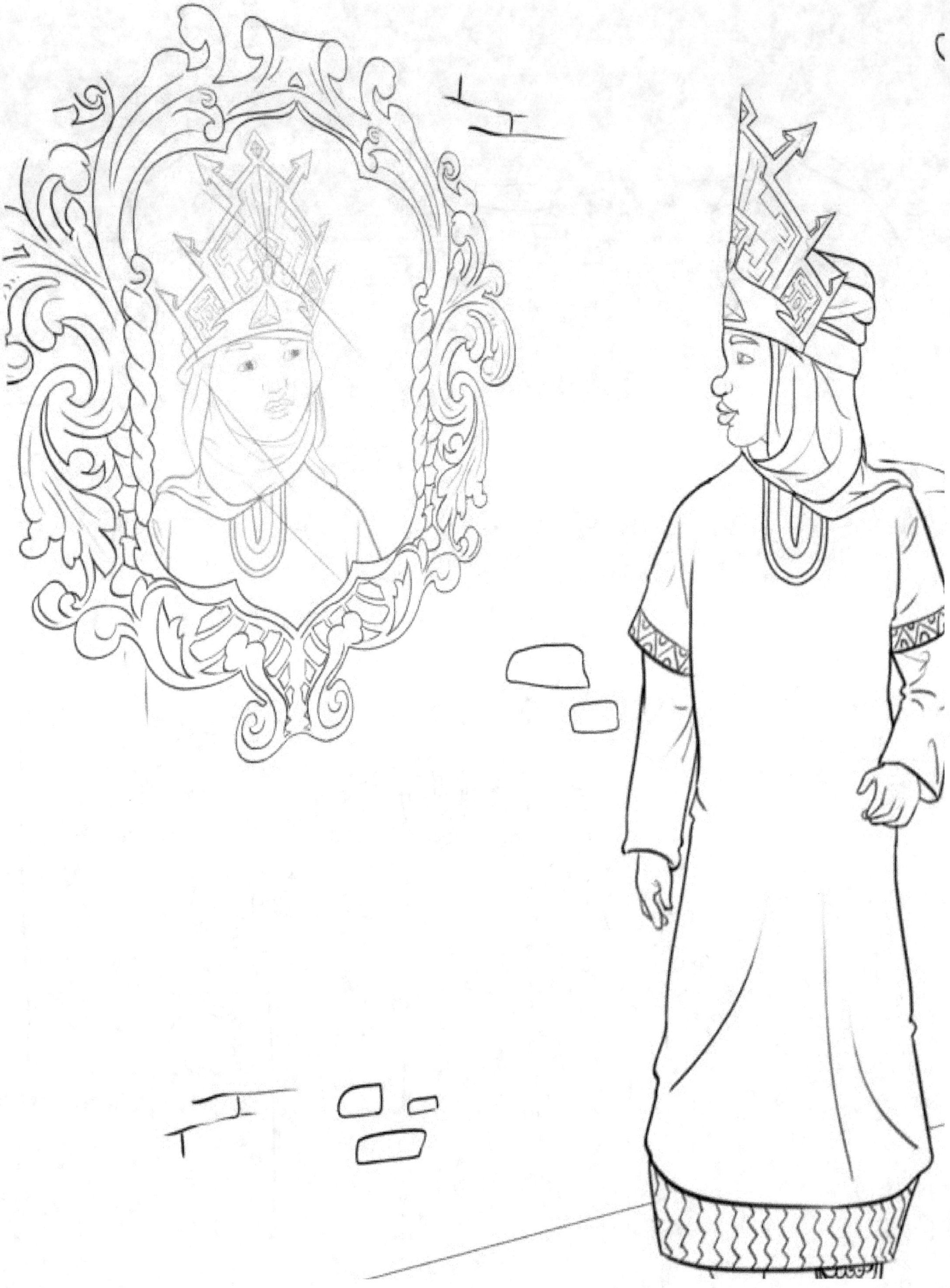

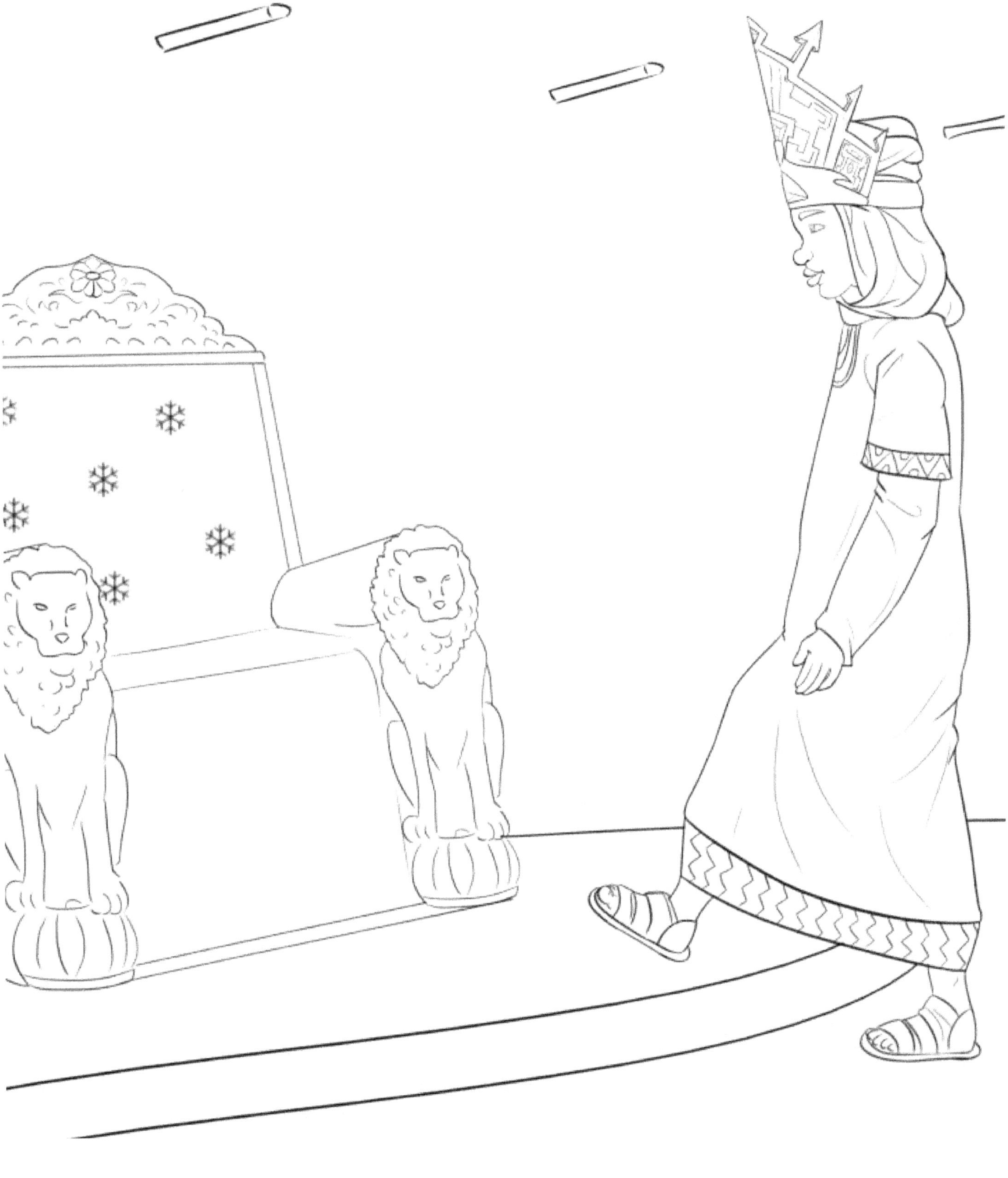

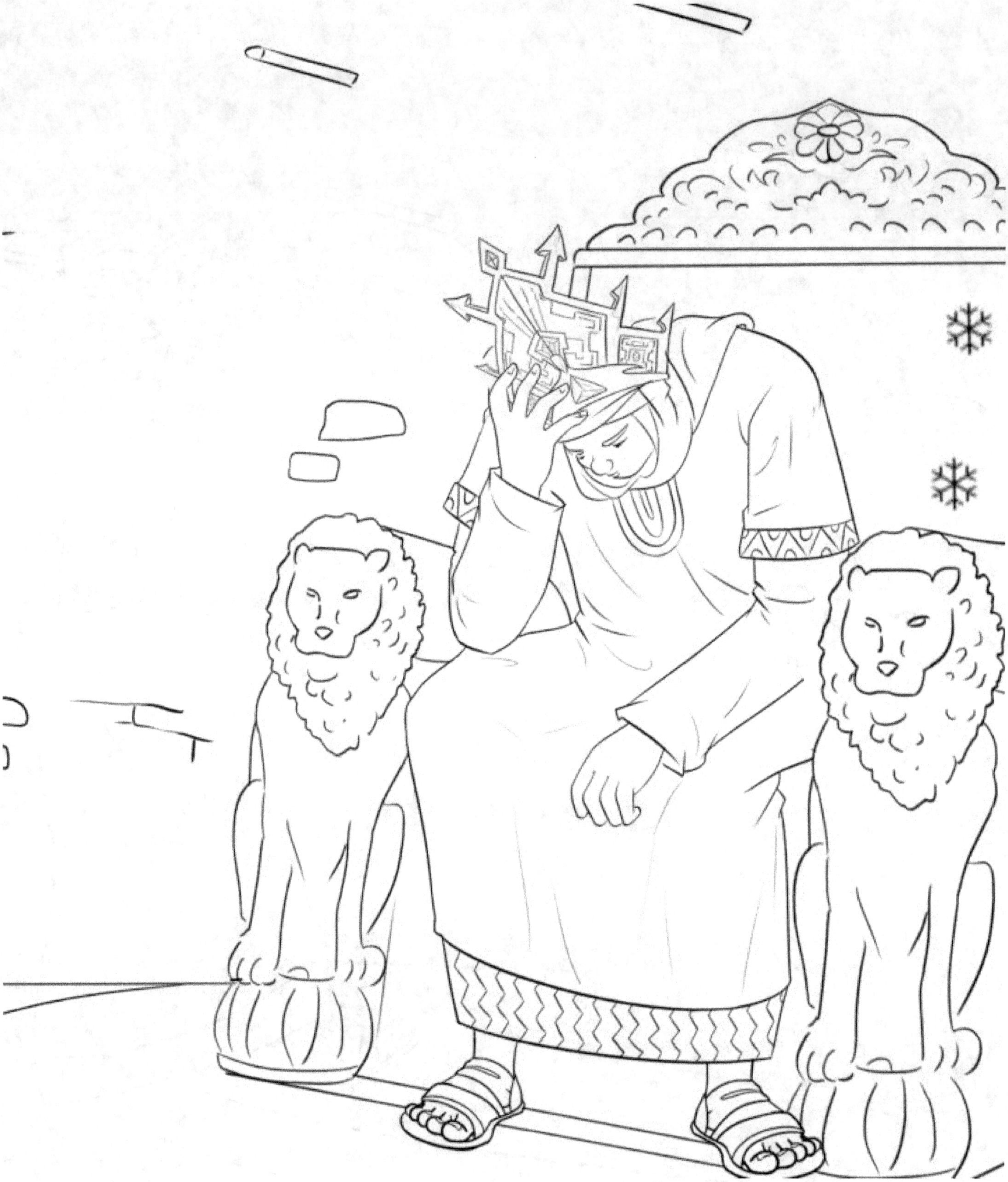

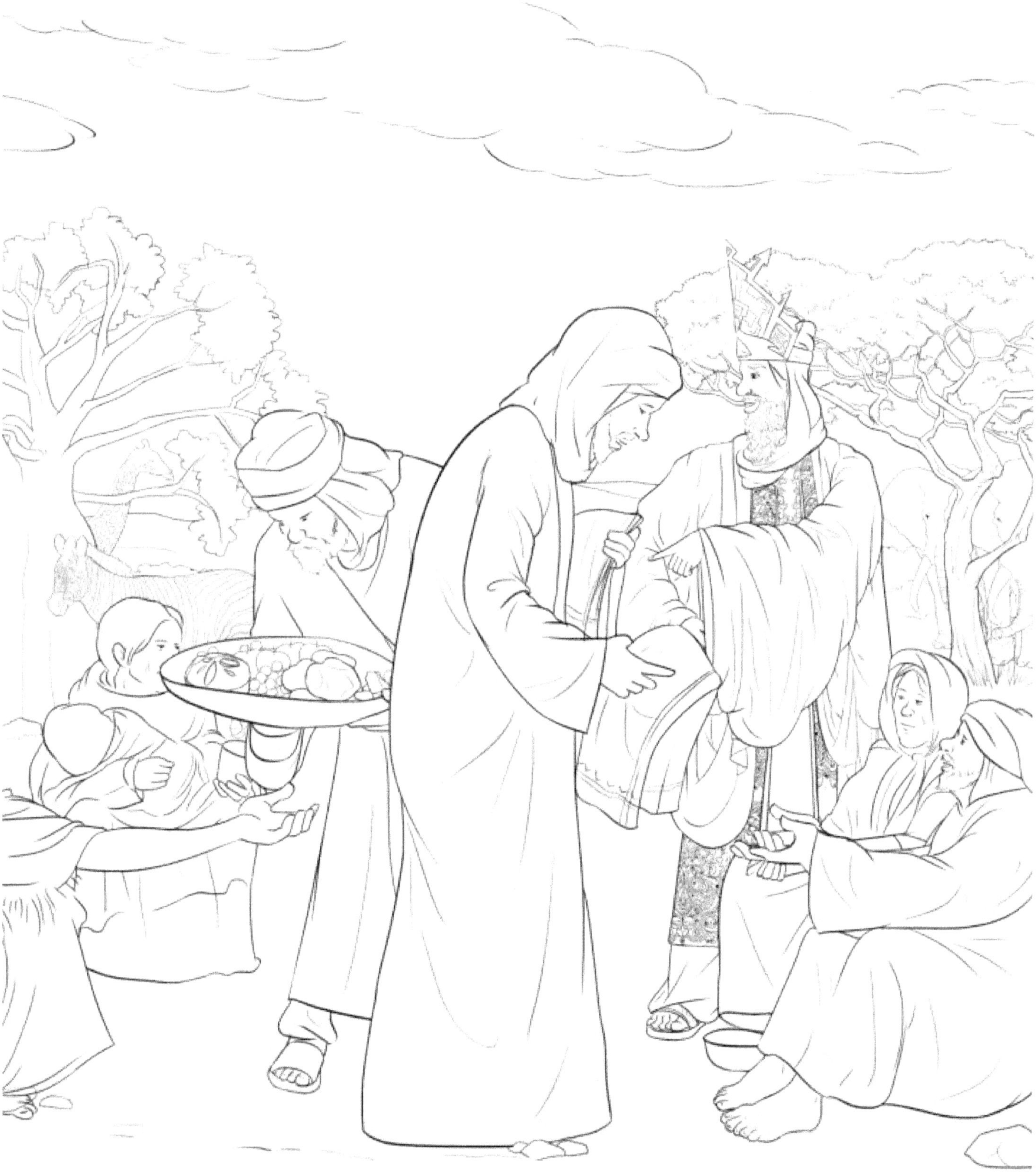

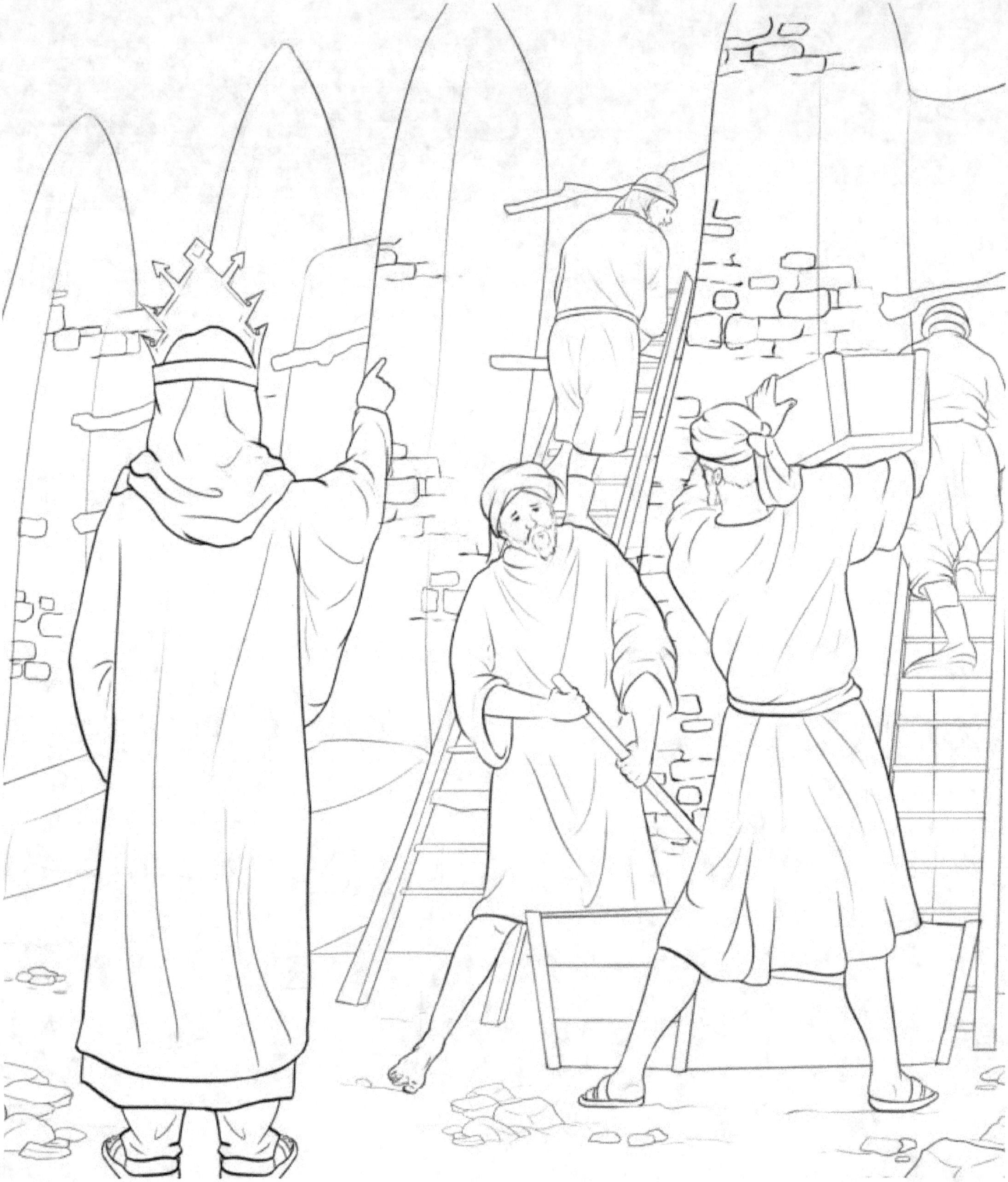

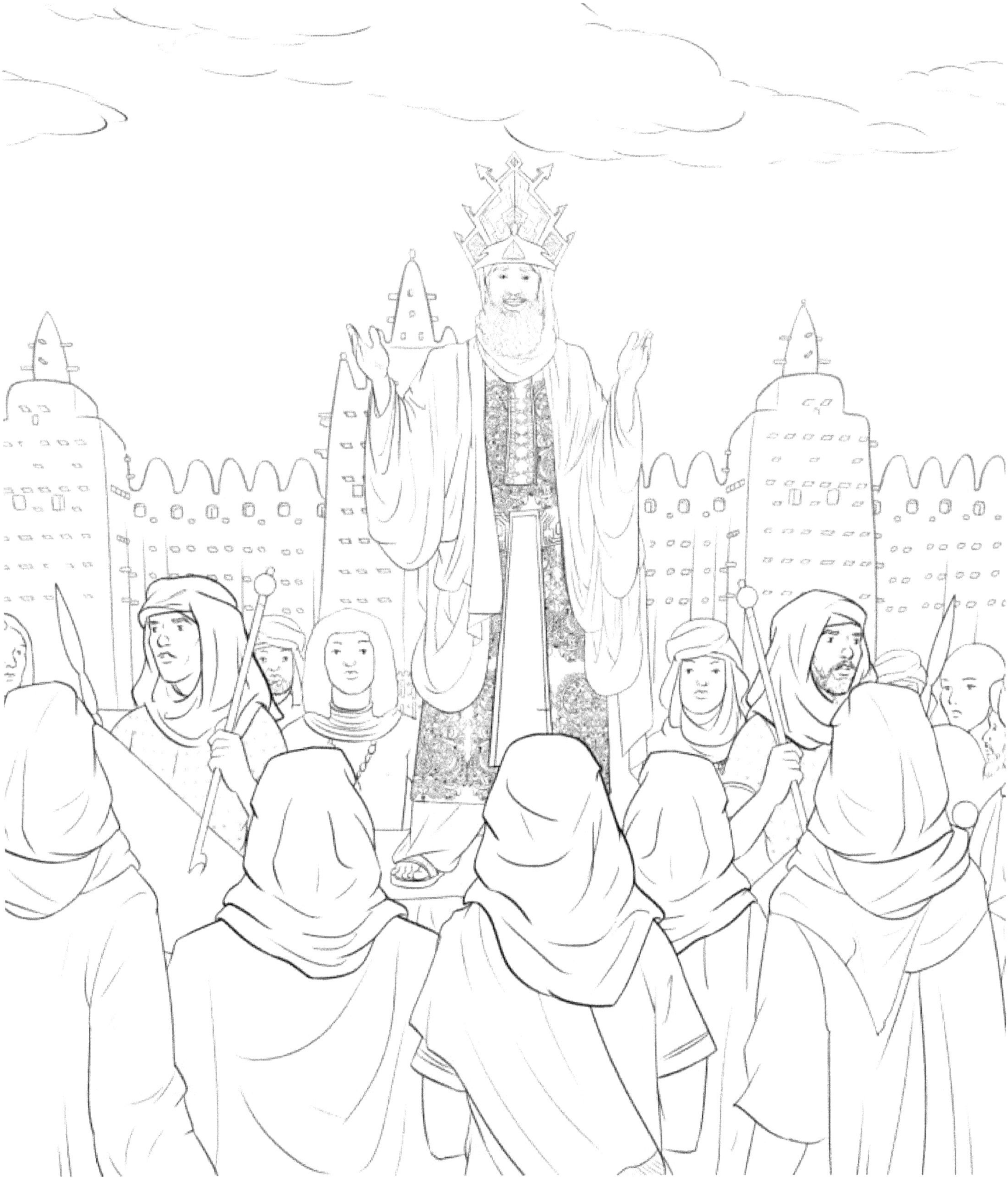

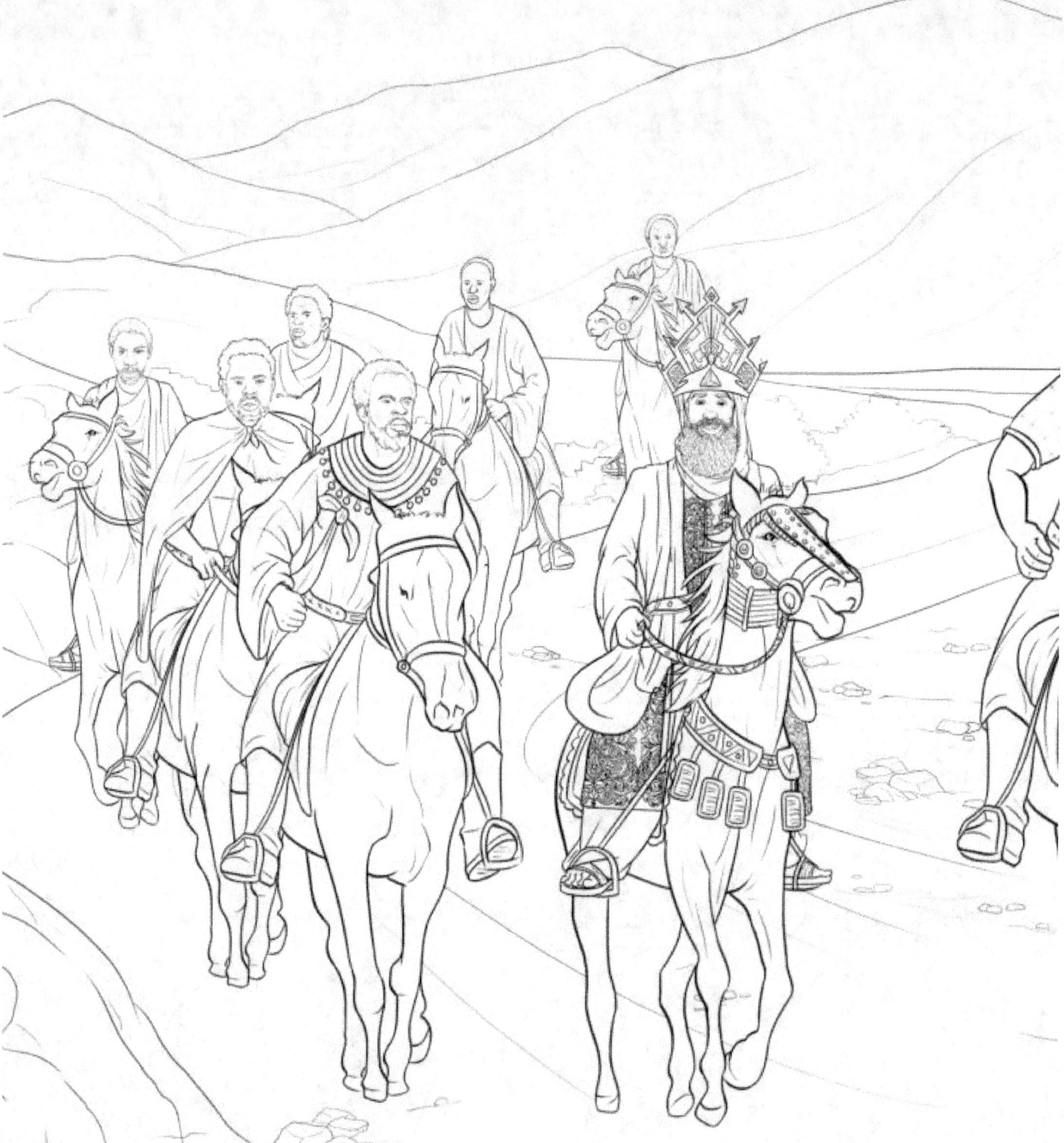

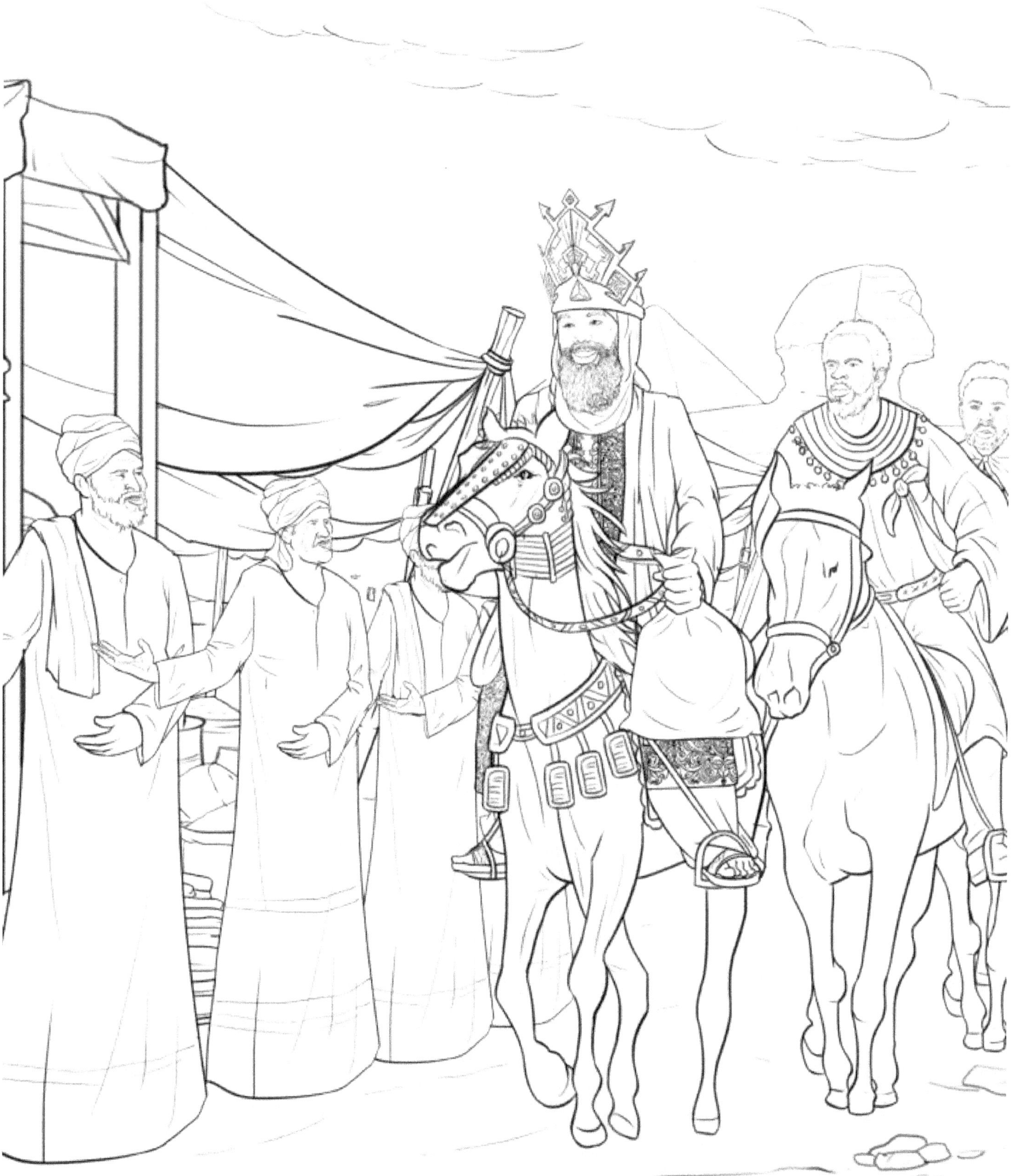

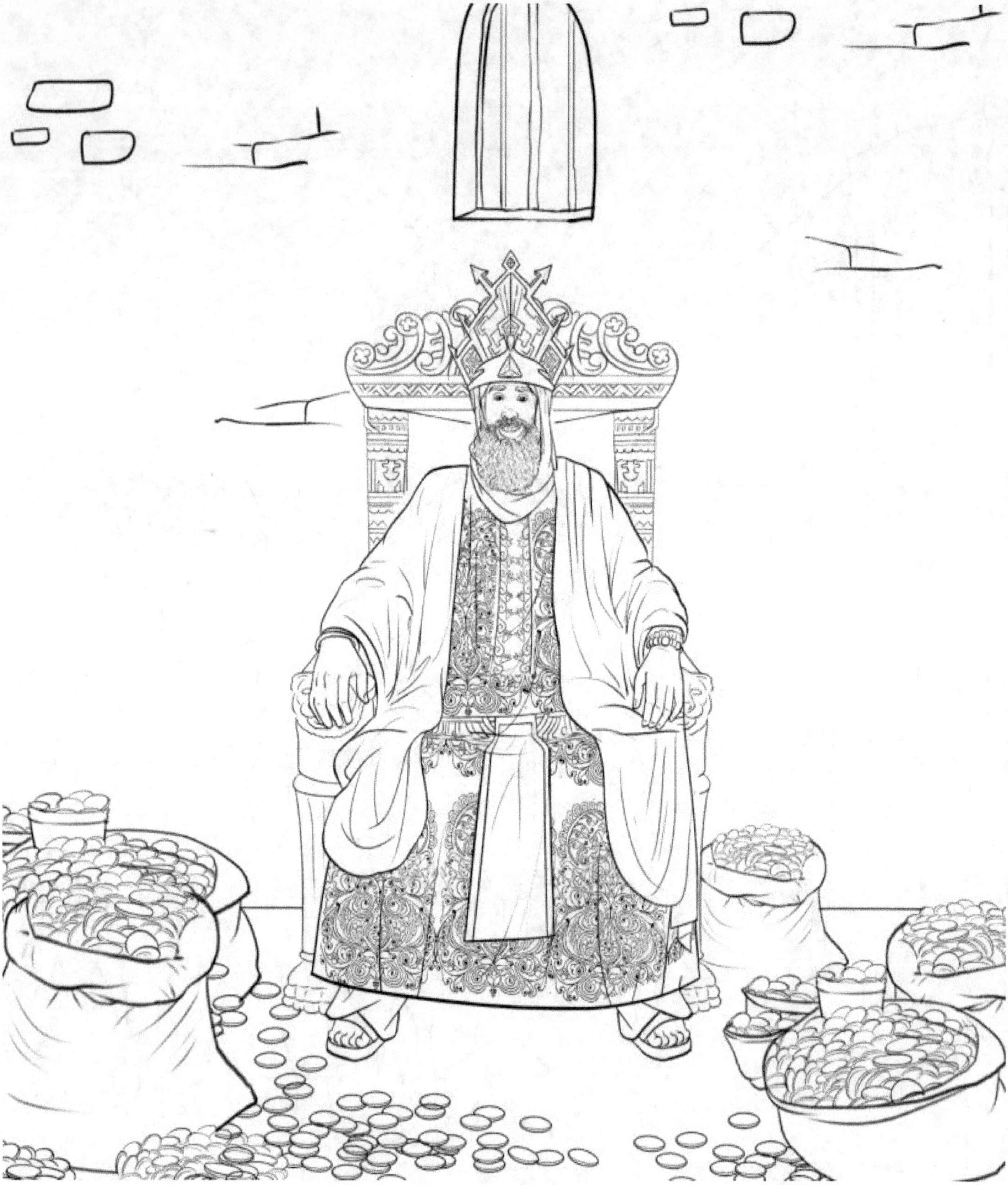

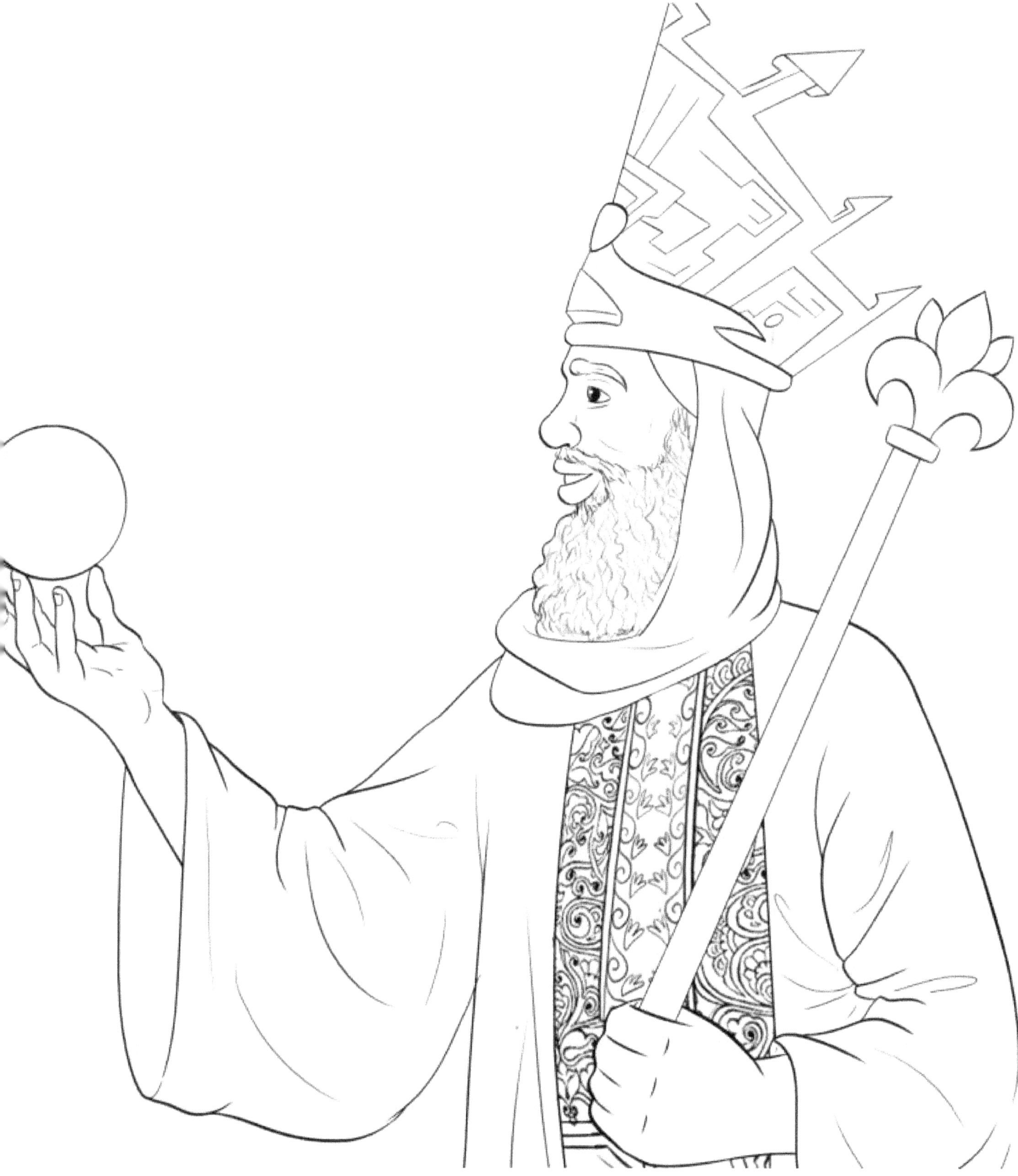

www.ingramcontent.com/pod-product-compliance
Lightning Source LLC
Chambersburg PA
CBHW080626220526
45467CB00011B/3388
* 9 7 9 8 7 1 3 0 7 0 2 4 3 *